Praise for Jeff Gundy's work...

Truly a wonderful book. The portrait of the speaker that emerges is one of a neighborly metaphysician, a deep, quirky, philosophical, humorous mind surveying the world and everything in it with great care, compassion, pity.
—LI-YOUNG LEE

Jeff Gundy isn't afraid of writing in the direction of the weird, strange, uncanny or odd —all words he isn't afraid to use in a poem either —nor does he fear writing directly toward beauty, truth and God.
—JULIA KASDORF

If Whitman were born in the Midwest to Mennonite parents, listened to Dylan and the Dead and loved to laugh at himself, he'd sound just like Jeff Gundy. His poetry reminds us, over and over, that paying attention to the delights and troubles of existence becomes a kind of psalm to this botched and beautiful creation.
—PHILIP METRES

Jeff Gundy writes immensely sane poetry made rarer by its simultaneous preservation of recklessness, surely one of poetry's primary tasks.
—DEAN YOUNG

I don't know how long it's been since I've read a book in which the author seemed to be so constantly in motion, so restless in his insatiable curiosity. How very attractive I find that, especially when it comes borne on genuine humility and unaffected generosity. This is a remarkable collection.
—TED KOOSER

Reading *Flatlands*, you feel the author's honesty palpably, his lack of side; these are genuine, searching poems, with no airs about them, full of wry wonder and warmth.
—JEAN VALENTINE

Inquiries possesses more theological curiosity than any book I've read in years, and Gundy engages his subjects with verve, wit, passion, and deep intelligence.
—ANDREW HUDGINS

What a delight it is to encounter the rich and compelling world of Jeff Gundy's *Flatlands*. These are poems of real vision and power, often darkly playful yet always resonant with both life's pleasures and its regrets.

—DAVID ST. JOHN

These vivid meditations call us to enter the whirl of our desires. With wit and passion, Jeff Gundy investigates our deep roots of longing for God and the other. He offers an unforgettable ride. In a voice both brave and tender he carries us through rain-streaked darkness and sun's glare towards love, towards those who call us to "bring yourself home."

—JEAN JANZEN

Just as a river finds inevitable kinship between remote hills and a distant sea, this book employs the prehensile reach of poetry to link local wisdom and distant war, to bind sacred callings and daily life.

—KIM STAFFORD

Impish, probing, and expansive, Gundy's poems reward the mind and replenish the spirit, speaking truth in the most human way.

—LYNN POWELL

Jeff Gundy *observes,* with a humble, winsome eye...and an ear for song. . . . What a joy it is to follow the trails he traces across the page—and out into the world.

—TERRY HERMSEN

BOOKS BY JEFF GUNDY

Poetry

Inquiries (Bottom Dog Press, 1992)
Flatlands (CSU Poetry Center, 1996)
Rhapsody with Dark Matter (Bottom Dog Press, 2000)
Deerflies (WordTech Editions, 2004)
Spoken Among the Trees (Akron University Press, 2007)
Somewhere Near Defiance (Anhinga Press, 2014)
Abandoned Homeland (Bottom Dog Press, 2015)
Without a Plea (Bottom Dog Press, 2019)

Poetry Chapbooks

Back Home in Babylon (Pinchpenny Press, 1974)
Johnny America Takes on Mother Nature (Pinchpenny Press, 1975)
Surrendering to the Real Things (Pikestaff Press, 1986)
Greatest Hits (Pudding House, 2003)

Prose

A Community of Memory: My Days with George and Clara (University of Illinois Press, 1996)
Scattering Point: The World in a Mennonite Eye (SUNY Press, 2003)
Walker in the Fog: On Mennonite Writing (Cascadia Press, 2005)
Songs from an Empty Cage: Poetry, Mystery, Anabaptism, and Peace (Cascadia Press, 2013)
Wind Farm: Landscape with Stories and Towers (Dos Madres Press, 2021)

Unpublished manuscripts

The Other Side of Empire (prose/poetry, ca. 2009)
The Traveler Ponders Some Rumors (poetry/prose, ca. 2016)

REPORTS FROM AN INTERIOR PROVINCE:
NEW & SELECTED POEMS

JEFF GUNDY

DOS MADRES
2025

DOS MADRES PRESS INC.
P.O. Box 294, Loveland, Ohio 45140
www.dosmadres.com   editor@dosmadres.com

Dos Madres is dedicated to the belief that the small press is essential to the vitality of contemporary literature as a carrier of the new voice, as well as the older, sometimes forgotten voices of the past. And in an ever more virtual world, to the creation of fine books pleasing to the eye and hand.

Dos Madres is named in honor of Vera Murphy and Libbie Hughes, the "Dos Madres" whose contributions have made this press possible.

Dos Madres Press, Inc. is an Ohio Not For Profit Corporation and a 501 (c) (3) qualified public charity. Contributions are tax deductible.

Executive Editor: Robert J. Murphy

Illustration & Book Design: Elizabeth H. Murphy
www.illusionstudios.net

Cover painting by Philip Sugden, "Doors of Perception" (2010)
Cover art photographer: Ron Pahl
Cover art from the collection of Sarah and Ryan Smith

Typeset in Adobe Garamond Pro & Garamond
ISBN 978-1-962847-24-7
Library of Congress Control Number: 2025934407

First Edition
Copyright 2025 Jeff Gundy
All rights reserved. No part of this book may be reproduced or transmitted in any form or by any means graphic, electronic or mechanical, including photocopying, recording, taping or by any information storage or retrieval system, without the permission in writing from the publisher.
Published by Dos Madres Press, Inc.

GRATITUDE

How to properly thank the great cloud of people who have contributed, in a myriad of ways, to the accumulation of all these poems, and many others omitted, abandoned, or forgotten along the way? Some must be named: Keith Ratzlaff, whose late advice on this book was crucial. Julia Kasdorf, and Jean Janzen, with Keith my first and closest friends among the scattered but vital tribe of Menno poets. Clint McCown, Don Morrill, Terry Hermsen, Julia Levine, Stephen Corey, Kevin Stein, and many other poet friends. My many fine colleagues at Bluffton University, including Susan Carpenter, Cindy Bandish, Lamar Nisly, Tobias Buckell, Perry Bush, and others past and present. Editors who saw earlier books into print, especially Larry Smith, Elton Glaser, and Robert Murphy. Too many journals and their editors to name. The ghosts of Walt Whitman, Emily Dickinson, William Blake, William Stafford, and innumerable other poets whose work echoes in my head. And of course my irreplaceable wife Marlyce, our grown sons Nate, Ben, and Joel, their wives Jessica, Jen, and Martha, and our lively set of grandchildren, who delight, exhaust, and inspire us all.

And if I think for a moment, I know the range of my gratitude should extend much further, to innumerable people, creatures, and things of this shining, tattered web in which we live and move and breathe. The people who made this country their home for millennia before mine came over the water. The men who built my old oak desk, those who picked beans for the coffee in my cup, those who tended the tree. And the tree, the soil, the water, the air.

CONTENTS

NEW POEMS

I.

Geese, Or The Way It Is in My Town 1
Bears 2
Varieties of Water, or Property 4
Criminal Justice in the Central Midwest 6
Notes from Bliss Hall, or How It's Going 8
Split in Three Movements 10
Some Naïve Questions 11
Notes Pertaining to the Tempest 13
Rumor of Wings 15

II.

Running across the Pews 19
Greasing the Plow 20
Submarine 21
Quicksilver Messenger Service, *Happy Trails* (1969) .. 23
Elegy for a Solid Man 25
September Lament 26
Ways to Fail to Change an American Mind, Even with a Solid
    Hook and a Bridge to Die For 28
Stairway 29

III.

Musclewood 33
Les Bar des PTT 35
Seven Ways into the Pond 37
Cornstalks 39
The Skink Poem 40
Afternoon with Wind, Brown Thrasher, and Dream of Flying .. 42
Kingfisher, or How Certain Autumn Days Advocate for a
    Significant Realignment of the Human Project 44

IV.

Reports from an Interior Province 49
Instructions for Surviving the Eclipse, the Merger, and the Flood 52
The Poet Resists His Own Instructions at the Nature Preserve. 54
Seven Ways of Looking at Raspberries 56
Wednesday at the Pond 58
Threshold Signal 60
Implicit Bias in the Wilds of Allen County 61
Clay into Birds 62

V.

Little Bridges 65
Sunday Morning at River Ridge Mansion 66
The Guy with the Pumpkin on His Head 68
Sunset Hill, Father's Day 69
Pura Vida at Tambor Beach 70
Phantom #9 73
Looking for the Path 74
Purple 76

INQUIRIES (1992)

Chainsaw Inquiries 81
Inquiries into the Technology of Hell and Certain Rumors
    Recently Circulating 82
Inquiries into the Technology of Beauty 84
Inquiry into the Discovery of the City into Which the Saints
    Have Been Said to Go, Marching 86
Inquiry into What One Can Do with a Rented Jackhammer 88
Inquiry into the Nature of Beauty, or the Tale of the King of
    the Cats 90
Inquiry into Gifts, or the Indigo Bunting 92

Flatlands (1995)

Where I Live 95
Knowing the Father 97
Squirrels 98
For the Soft God Paula 100
"The Universe Is a Safe Place for Souls" 102
Where I Grew Up 103
Walking Beans 105
His Name Was Gerdon and He Ran a Hatchery
    in Graymont, Illinois 107
Seams 109

Rhapsody with Dark Matter (2000)

Rain 113
Hunger 114
Breakfast at the County Seat Café 115
The Sadness of Water and Women 116
Old Water 119
Rhapsody with Dark Matter 121
The Little Clerk 122
The Cookie Poem 124
How the Boy Jesus Resisted Taking Out the Trash . . . 126
Ancient Themes #1: The Martyrs & the Child 127
The Black Father 129
Letter to J. from the Ramada Inn Western Avenue, Albany 131
What the Prairie Boy Learned on the Whistler Road 136

Greatest Hits (2003)

The Archetypal Experience of C. Wordsworth Crockett 139
How to Write the New Mennonite Poem 141

Deerflies (2004)

Deerfly 145
Mumble 146
Black Cat in Byhalia 147
Meditation in Glen Helen 150
White Dog 152
Morning Song from Oneonta 154
Instructions for the Night Walk 156
Ancient Themes: The First Teacher 158
Second Morning Song from Oneonta 159
Brain Remembers Things That Did Not Happen ... 160
Epiphany with Sirens and White-Tail 161
Letter from Ragdale to J. 162
Scenario 164
Ancient Themes: The Spring at Ragdale 165
Ancient Themes: The Night 166
Small Night Song from Oneonta 167

Spoken among the Trees (2007)

Damselfly 171
Fulks Run to Cumberland 172
Advice for Walkers 173
The Recovery of Imaginary Friends 175
Late Psalm 176
Interior Colloquy in Glen Helen 178
Ode to Luna with Implausible Quotations 179
February Report on Conditions in the Interior ... 180
Where Water Finds an Edge 182
Firefly 183
When Madonna Met Menno 184
Letter with Melody and Fall from Chair 185
The Song of the Weed Witch 186
Report on Recent Activities in Austin (Selected) .. 188
Lunch Poem at Snow Road 190

Contemplation with Ledges and Moon 192
From the Screen Porch 194
Spring Tractates 195
Contemplation at the Bar R Ranch 200
"Night, the Astonishing . . ." 201

The Other Side of Empire (ca. 2009)

Translation 205
Damp Ode 206

Somewhere Near Defiance (2014)

Somewhere Near Defiance 211
Meditation with Wallet, Eyeglasses, and Little Riley Creek 214
Autobiography with *Blonde on Blonde* 216
Interior Housekeeping 217
No Path 218
Having It All Four Ways 219
Meditation with Muddy Woods and Swinging Bridge ... 222
Slippers 224
On the Birthday of Ronald Reagan and My Mother-in-Law,
    I Mourn Jerry Garcia 225
The Unreliable Narrator Remembers the *Martyrs Mirror*
    Conference 227
Contemplation with Rainy Birdsong 230
Contemplation on Rules and Lines 231
Contemplation on Rain and Religion 232
Something the Winter Wren Didn't Say 233
Evening with Long Books 234
Oh 236
Notes from the Faculty Meeting 238
Additional Assertions on Soul 239
On the Way to the Glacier 240
Meditation in Glen Park with Springs and Bad News 242

The Traveler Ponders Some Rumors (ca. 2016)

The Traveler Ponders Some Rumors
    That Have Reached His Ears 247
Windy Walk with Espresso and Globalization 248
Windy Walk with Hooded Crows 250
Things Overheard, Observed, and Possibly Misunderstood 251
The Indolent Professor Is Shamed into Uncertain Epiphany 253
Palanga Stintas 255
The Traveler Attends the Friday Evening Concert 257
The Traveler Encounters More Renowned Cities, Foreign
    Tongues, and Items of Historical Significance 259
The Traveler Fails Kierkegaard Once and for All 266

Abandoned Homeland (2015)

The Body. 269
Contemplation with Old Honda, Carnality, Fish 271
Reading Neil Gaiman in a Western Suburb 273
Thread 275
Safety 276
Ode with Winter Sunshine, One Mind, Four Houses 278
Contemplation with Acorns and Guitar 279
Cookies 281
Letter from an Ohio Classroom 283
Fifty Billion Planets 285
Abandoned Homeland of Exiles 287
Three for Trakl 288
Ambitions 290
The Mysteries in Yellow Springs 291
Meditation on Narrative, Dogma, and Flight 293
Brief History of Midwestern Civilization 294
Further Notes on the Martyrs 295
Something Is 297
Waterfall 298

Without a Plea (2019)

Plain Advice 303
Late Summer with Mink, Duende, and Calamities
    of Varying Degree 304
"Nothing Is Level There" 306
Mud and Gravel 308
Further Inquiries into Duende 311
The Listener at the Conference on Peacebuilding,
    or Playing the Spider 313
God Is Not Right, He Is Big 315
Elegy in Two Places and Two Parts 317
The God of Dirt 319
Where I Was Instead 320
Late Spring in Old River Town with Guesswork and
    Bombay Sapphire Gin 322
Determinism on a Summer Morning in the Midwest 324
Zen & Blacktop 328
Traces 330
On the Way to Denver 332
Late Explanation 333
Soft Tissue 335
On the Condition of Rural America 336
The Smaller Mysteries on a Winter Sunday Morning 338
Some Sentences for a Man Who Won't Read Them 340
Nice People 342
Tablets 344
Lessons of a Gentle Childhood 345

About the Author 347
Acknowledgements 349

NEW POEMS

Geese, Or The Way It Is in My Town

> *You do not have to be good . . .*
>   - Mary Oliver, "The Wild Geese"

True. But pretending to be good
keeps things easier in a village like mine,
a quiet place with three decent restaurants,

all walkable. High school basketball
is the main thing, except for football.
The good citizens drive large trucks

and larger SUVs, display strange flags
and ominous signs. The God they worship
is always looking for enemies to drown.

And yes, the geese—they graze in the parks,
crap anywhere, float wherever they please
in their honky arrogance. Care nothing

for what other creatures might want, or need.
They defend their young fiercely, hissingly.
They know the law is on their side.

Bears

> *And some folks even see the bear in me.*
> -Steven Fromholz, "Bears"

Do you want to see bears, our host asked, and No I said at once,
I have no desire to get mauled, but the very next day we saw

a grizzly in the lake. It climbed the bank as the boat veered close,
rose up on the steep shore like an elemental, vanished.

And that night a black bear tipped off the lid of the can
by the garage, found nothing tempting, wandered on.

I will not say more of them, or the cabin without running water
with many old sitcoms on DVD, or the cabin with the awkward

noisy staircase. I must tell how my father took it on himself to die
four days into the trip, two days after we saw him miserable

in the care home, saying *Do you trust these people?* and *Can I please
take off this shirt? Please?* We got the call as we fought a hot headwind

into South Dakota, too late to turn back, too late for everything,
and so he haunted the highway all the way to Billings, to Boise,

to Golden, haunted the mountains he never saw in his ninety years,
traveled with us like the bear bell I clipped to the day pack.

It chimed and clinked unsteadily as we trudged and clambered,
a fragile ward against danger, one that either worked or served

only to jingle us on our way. I looked for bears black and grizzled
every two to twenty minutes but never had to pull the clumsy cylinder

of bear spray from its place. Anyway I could not imagine
that I could save myself or anyone from the smallest, tamest bear

with such a flimsy ward, with no training in its use. But we heard
only the bear bell, saw only scat, and at last I knew I had not

spoken truly, I wanted to see bears and live, to be among those
who have seen bears and ghosts, who have a story to tell.

Varieties of Water, or Property

1.
The blackberry canes tug at my sleeve, not
because they like me. The low spot I tried

did indeed get my feet wet. Two geese
complain on the new ice skinning the pond,

fly when they see me. At the bridge
there's mist above the creek, old ice,

new ice, flowing water in amongst it all.
Tiny bubbles cling to the fine branch-tips,

half melted, ready to let go. *Otherworldly*
I write but no, this is precisely worldly.

2.
I stand in the trees for who knows how long,
the path lost, indecisive, almost happy.

And then a man approaches, and when
he gets close he says *This is my property,*

and the next pond is John's property, and John
will shoot you, and I might have shot you.

3.
I thank him for not shooting me,
ask his advice about the best way back.

You could ask John about walking his land, he says.

4.
I go back the way I came, through mist,
over the crunchy melting ground,

soggy leaves, iced-over puddles,
the creek still telling its endless story.

So many varieties of water, all of them free,
all of them not free at all.

Criminal Justice in the Central Midwest

> *American poetry voluntarily turned itself in. Tate and*
> *Ransom went through town after town asking, 'Does anyone*
> *know of a good jail near here?"*
> —Robert Bly, "Looking for Dragon Smoke"

1.
My home town had no jail, no station, just one cop in a cruiser,
his only duty to harass us high school kids, who were also

driving around in cars we didn't own. Gas was cheap. Wild waves
of music rolled down from Chicago: the Stones, the Animals.

We gotta get out of this place. Friday nights we drove to Pontiac,
cruised the courthouse. Mr. Quick's had 29¢ burgers. Now and then

a fight, a girl named Nicki who'd talk to anybody. Mostly we got tired,
the gas ran low, we drifted home. Kids like us are still dreaming

of escape, bored, wired, and ignorant as the power lines that dipped
and rose, carried heat and light into our cramped bedrooms,

into classrooms where we sulked and brooded, sneered
at our teachers, peered sideways at girls in their minimal skirts.

2.
Pontiac had a real prison, still does, Level One, 2000 souls stuck
behind steel and concrete. The big riot flared in July '78—

three officers dead, buildings ash and rubble. When they finally got
the place locked down, they slammed everyone into deadlock

for three full months. No showers, no exercise, no phone calls.
The governor tried to close it down in '08, but the locals

protested, fiercely. Biggest employer in the county.

3.
I escaped. College and on into grad school. Built trailers
for summer money, read sad and rowdy poets, learned new words

and worlds. I loved how Bly mocked those stiff old Southerners.
But now, home to visit, I walk the streets of my beat-up village,

past the weary small houses and shuttered Ford place,
past the empty restaurant and the last open bar. And it seems

I see two weary men in dusty suits, tapping on door after door,
asking every stranger where they might rest for the night.

Notes from Bliss Hall, or How It's Going

1.
Consider the muse as garter snake, curling gentle at the edge of the path. Or don't.

Consider the 18-foot Burmese python that three trained men struggled to pin down and overcome in the Everglades. They found 132 eggs inside her, and a half-digested young white-tail.

Consider the python's four-times-or-so grandmother, trapped in some Burmese jungle, shipped across the Pacific and the continent to be sold for a hundred bucks from somebody's van, dumped in a ditch when she outgrew her cage.

Consider her spectacular how-many-times granddaughter—another hard-working refugee turned successful immigrant and apex predator, scouring the swamp for any breathing thing, squeezing, breaking, swallowing.

Consider this one more fucked-up late capitalist quasi-parable, one more slide into the swamp of hunger, sex, dread, half a man's face peeled by a lashing tail.

Consider those 132 eggs, crushed, seeping into a soggy hummock.

Consider the white-tails, the raccoons and possums and foxes, if any are left, for the mother and her kin are so very hungry, so good at what they do.

2.
Consider that in the interests of fictional justice, the high-minded Atticus Finch wrenched and twisted something like the truth from his crucial witness, a poor girl who was not in

fact raped by a black man. May Ewell is her name, but I had to look it up. She only has the one big scene, where she's forced into shamed revelation. Her father made her do it.

Justice was not served anyway, in this particular fiction. Did Bob Ewell think his hapless daughter would hold tight against a well-dressed, clever white man, when all her life he'd demanded she obey or get smacked? Can we imagine anything for her but one hard man after another?

3.
Consider Grendel's mother crashing the mead-hall, furious, grieving her slaughtered son, slaughtering the gathered warriors in her fury, so that the great hero must find her cave below the bloody, burning lake, must don his chain-mail and dive, must be seized and nearly crushed. Only with her own ancient, heavy sword may he slash her nearly in two.

4.
Consider these mothers, these daughters. Why are they so hungry, so angry? Why must they trouble us so? If they were not so hungry, not so angry, we could forgive them.

Split in Three Movements

> *Or like a stairway to the sea,*
> *Where down the blind are driven.*
>   -E. A. Robinson, "Eros Turannos"

1.
History is annoying, Lucia said. *We learn nothing,*
yet we do the wars again. Our guide to Split, she was
a child during the war. *And now, now here they go again,*
she said as she led us through Diocletian's palace.
He stabilized the empire, raised taxes, tried and failed
to kill off the Christians. Then strangely he retired
to his giant palace, grew cabbages. Then the empire
turned Christian and complications ensued,
as we all know. The good people of Split bent
to the Venetians, Austria-Hungary, Mussolini, Tito.
This is not a complete or precise history,
but Lucia kept walking, and I took no notes.

2.
The stairway to the sea remains, weathered
but usable, and a man comes down it daily
to smoke and ponder the unsettled waters.
The waves mutter, the limestone cliffs climb
to meet the plane trees, lush and green,
the abandoned cola factory, the harbor
tower and the bell tower behind.
Two lovers help each other down the steps.

3.
History is annoying, Lucia said, and it seemed
she might speak of her losses, her grief,
but no. We stood on the ancient stones,
thirty strangers to her and to each other.
The tour was over and she thanked us
and we clapped a little and some of us
tipped her, and elsewhere the wars went on.

Some Naïve Questions
(Exodus 14 and 15)

1. If the Israelites were already out of town, why would God bother to harden Pharoah's heart?
2. Describe the precise sort of glory that results from a vastly superior being manipulating the natural world to slaughter an entire army, complete with chariots and horses.
3. Just how culpable were the horses?
4. Might drowning a smaller number of men and/or horses have sufficed to convince the Egyptians that the Lord is mighty in battle?
5. Did Pharoah drown along with his army, and if so, was his successor established when the waters swept over him?
6. On which shore were the dead deposited, or were some on either side?
7. If not one member of the army survived, how long did it take for the Egyptians to discover them?
8. How accurate was the expectation that once the Egyptian soldiers (and horses) were washed up with their lungs full of the Red Sea, the mothers and fathers and wives and children left behind would worship and fear the God of Israel?
9. Would a discussion of "worship" and "fear" as related but not identical terms be useful here?
10. In light of all these events, how exactly would you define "unfailing love"?
11. Which of the participants in this narrative might seem most sympathetic to contemporary audiences, depending on their particular contexts?
12. How might this narrative be read by a) the spiritual descendants of those who fled Pharoah's army; b) citizens of the planet's most powerful nation, supplier of massive weaponry to the

spiritual descendants of those who fled Pharoah's army; c) the inhabitants of an impoverished, walled enclave now largely destroyed by the spiritual descendants of those who fled Pharoah's army?

13. Which category most closely describes you?

14. Are these appropriate questions? Why or why not?

15. Having contemplated this narrative and the songs of Moses and Miriam, do you find yourself a) desiring to sing praises to the Lord, who is highly exalted; b) terrified; c) seized by a mysterious trembling; d) other? Please explain.

Notes Pertaining to the Tempest

Why is this beautiful? Christian asks. How do you decide
on the six most beautiful cemeteries in the world?
He speaks of Magellan, of narrow waters, of time

and coins, errors and bones of the disappeared:
we must coin a more vast, luminous, and plural memory.
And Ellen speaks of the Utrecht Psalter, rivers

flowing from paradise, elephants and dragons.
Both evil and comedy were real in those days.
People *wanted* true stories. It has never been easy.

And the violin came at the same time, Jim says,
while the bold explorers rode the waves into new lands—
yes, new to them. It takes a big tree and centuries

to make a double bass. When stories are lost,
the whole society is wounded. And the Spanish burned
the Mayan Codices, because God, because they could.

And Brazil outlawed slavery only in 1888, says Camilla.
Coffee, sugar cane, pineapple. Those outlandish early maps,
giant insects and monsters, mirrors of fears and desires.

And photos: men climbing a cliff, packed close as bees.
Might our forgotten thoughts be adapted by others, passing by?
In 1800 Alexander von Humboldt saw it: the world

is a great web! He wrote forty brilliant books—
Thoreau and Whitman read him, the Brits too.
Yet even today some of us hate dandelions,

some don't. They are immigrants, but they make food
for bees, shine golden in their time, do little harm.
Without flowers, we'd none of us be here.

I am learning: you can try hard to love your home,
learn all you can, and still have it fall to ruin around you.
When the smoke moves south, the borders mean nothing.

Rumor of Wings

1.
The last high dive in Allen County has been torn down.
But the stations are bursting with gasoline,

roller hot dogs, Red Bull, twelve kinds of jerky.
The roads out of town are clear all four ways.

2.
Once I became a speck of light—no, I saw
in the shimmery mist a host of lights

that did not burn or cease to burn.
I went back to my wife and my children

and I told them nothing, I told
them nothing. I don't know why.

3.
Now I only want to spin skeins of sound
from the old guitar, sift and sort for some

new music, old as Jesus, young as Jesus.

4.
That night something came flying,
a gift in the shape of a cardinal or crow,

sharp in the shadowy darkness,
quiet as the rumor of wings.

5.
I woke into my life. I rose and dressed, ate,
like a criminal whose crime has been forgotten.

Running across the Pews

Just once during a potluck I went upstairs with some
of my friends, our parents still nibbling and chatting

in the basement, and it must have been winter because
we ran around the square plain sanctuary as though

it was a playground. We discovered that we could run
across the tops of the pews, they were spaced a longish

but not impossible distance apart, it was fun and not
even really scary to stride from the front to the back,

with the comforting padded seats promising a soft-ish
landing if a foot slipped. But when I turned and started

back I saw instead the hard backs of the pews and
the floor a goodly way down, if I missed a step

the landing would hurt plenty. I kept going, of course,
not because anybody was watching but because

I was bent on finishing. I was alert but not panicky,
pretty sure I could do this, I made the little leaps

as though my stumpy legs were born for nothing
more than leaping from pew to pew, day into month

into year, making the good landing or the hard one.

Greasing the Plow

> *No wonder of it: shéer plód makes plough down sillion*
> *Shine, and blue-bleak embers, ah my dear,*
> *Fall, gall themselves, and gash gold-vermilion.*
> —Gerard Manley Hopkins, "The Windhover"

> *Sillion is usually called the slice or furrow-slice . . . . When freshly cut a plastic soil with a high clay content does take on a sheen and, from a distance, the whole field may gleam for a while in low sunshine.*
> —Farm Direct UK

My father rarely worshipped using words, though he never
skipped church even to finish picking corn. He taught

mostly just by showing, kept a bucket with grease
and an old paintbrush to paint the plowshares

and rolling coulters so they wouldn't rust over the winter,
a good job after school for the boy I was, in dirty coveralls

and floppy yellow gloves. It was strangely satisfying
to smear the heavy, smelly, brown grease across

the shiny steel, get it smooth and even, seal the polished
curves and edges from the air. Next fall I backed

the tractor to the plow, hitched up the lift arms,
plugged in the hydraulics, drove from shed to field,

dropped the plow, felt it bite into the soil. The first earth
scoured the shares clean and I pulled the throttle open,

blasted slowly down the field, hid away the cornstalks
and bean stubble, turned the black soil in flat thick slices,

saw it break and steam and shine in the blaze of fall sun.

Submarine

The world is thick and deep, not quiet, not asleep.
It shows us only what we can learn to see.

This morning I spoke to an old friend who shook
his head, *This year's been rough,* he said, *I want*

to keep making things, but . . . He looked down,
gestured at his body. I knew what he meant.

We have to think of being, not making, I said,
and he looked at me sideways and then we both

laughed and sighed, knowing how easy that is to say.
And so he told me how way back in his Navy days

he'd been on duty, tracking Russian subs, when
far away one exploded underwater. They brought in

a giant crane, he said, hoisted up the whole front half,
recovered two nuclear-tipped torpedoes,

a control panel, and six drowned Russian sailors.
The Navy buried the sailors at sea. They filmed

the ceremony and sent it to Moscow, as evidence.

Somehow this story pleased us both. We did
not ask if the truth is like a buried submarine.

Why do I remember so much from sixty years ago,
he said, *when I have no idea where my keys are?*

And what if the truth is scattered as we are, lost like
the keys, stuck like half a submarine on the sea-floor

or afloat like a great balloon, the wind hard again
from the west today, branches waving

and recovering, blossoms losing their grip
and joining the current, tumbling, unafraid?

—for Lynn Miller

Quicksilver Messenger Service, Happy Trails (1969)

A 28-minute live version of "Who Do You Love" fills the whole first side of *Happy Trails*, energetic, earnest, redundant. Albums had sides then, and vinyl has come back, though my turntable is still moldering away in the basement.

Who do I love? Who do you? So much swirling everywhere, masked, unmasked, invisible and potent as the wind.

Bo Diddley did it first, 1957, rock just starting to roll, a snappy 2:29 radio song in the great tradition of the brag: he walked 47 miles of barbed wire, had a house made of rattlesnake hide, a skull for the chimney . . . *Now come on take a walk with me, Arlene, and tell me, who do you love?*

Later, Ronnie Hawkins wailed through it with the Band, who had left him far behind but brought him back for *The Last Waltz*.

My mother, also Arlene, was in her mid-twenties in 1957, already pregnant for the third time. I was five. Not her kind of song, but she's pushing 90 now and still tough as Bo. She's inside most of the time anyway, taking care of Dad, driving him to doctors, stopping at Wal-Mart for milk and buns and Kraft singles. The grocery in town mostly sells liquor and snacks these days, but there's a new Dollar General with a big food section. Of course there is.

In the sixties we poured mercury into our palms when we could get it, from the chem lab or a broken thermometer. That squish, the way it split and then sucked itself together. That shine.

We said *cool* and *far out*. Now I hear *Word. FTW. Drip.* Why not.

Just a hundred miles from my home town to the city. It always seemed another country, we went only to see the White Sox and the

Field Museum. But we found the Chicago stations, WLS, WMAQ, scratchy AM on little transistors, the world sneaking into our drafty farmhouse in a low-cut red dress. She Loves You. House of the Rising Sun. Eve of Destruction. Beauty and death and danger. Somehow our parents let us listen, and it changed us, not all in the same way.

Quicksilver will kill you, but what did we know? Some of us are gone, bad hearts, drugs, cancer, but those curious pools in our palms spared us, just as the rider with his bags of mail on the album cover never looked back but hurried down the dusty trail, last night's woman waving as his pony kicked up dust.

Elegy for a Solid Man

Surely there are enough fallen leaves, slippery in the cold woods,
acorn caps and sticks among them, mud and stone below,

a few still trembling on their branches like John M. in church
before his Parkinson's got so bad it kept him home. Sometime

in the middle of his struggle he sent me an angry bitter lament
he'd written. All I could think to do was thank him. John was

a big man, craggy, quiet. He sold milking equipment,
let his son run the farm. For a while he carried a big oak staff,

as if to beat it back. I'd see him rise for the prayer, leaning
on his stick, his head bowed, trembling only a little. Later

he told me he'd gotten past anger, apologized for what he'd written.
He was shaking more by then. I had, and have, no idea

whether rage or resignation is better. I told him not to worry.
I should have said I was proud he'd thought me worthy

to read such a thing, but in my tribe we just mutter and hope
it's enough. The sun is almost warm but low, 4:15, late January,

it catches a few leaves and they glow and the others wait,
not better or worse for not being tricked out by the light.

September Lament

1.
"Hey! Pole Barns!" says the lumberyard billboard.
But soon only the swaybacked barns, the sheds with splintered
    roofs, will have lightning rods.
Bill is now in palliative care, Sharon wrote from the island.
I'm sick of writing elegy, sick that Susan was too hazy to come with
    me, sick of the fires and droughts and hurricanes, weary
    of the glorious shimmers of light through the trees that
    remain.
Somehow I found myself on a causeway that curved for miles over
    the bay, like a ramp to heaven or to Marblehead.
The world is primarily a moral order, wrote Pirsig in his second
    book, the one nobody reads.
Electrons sometimes veer *inside* of protons, which are mostly
    empty anyway.
There's water on an earthlike planet 110 light years away.
How can we know so much about things great and small and still
    fuck up the whole world?
How can Bill the indestructible, who drank more casual Dewars on
    a slow afternoon than I could in three wild nights, be laid
    out flat in his late, Gandalfian beard?

2.
When did they stop putting lightning rods on houses?
Lightning strikes cause $1 billion damage a year in the U.S.
The Empire State Building is struck by lightning every other week,
    more or less.
A new system, I read, will redirect lightning with powerful lasers.
Another new system will redirect cancer into whitetails and
    starlings, two species in need of some culling. Someday,
    mosquitos.
Another new system will redirect all our stupidity, greed and self-
    sabotage into cost-effective and efficient action for the
    benefit of all.

The laser system is entirely speculative and faces major practical
> issues, if you think about it.
Planting a few billion trees might be easier.
Another new system . . . ah, enough.
Despite every system, Susan was not in the car with me, and she
> is not camped now at her favorite window in the big old
> house but stuck back in Yellow Springs, her mind like
> one of those airy protons, open so wide that any curious
> electron can glide through quick and graceful as a swallow.

Ways to Fail to Change an American Mind, Even with a Solid Hook and a Bridge to Die For

Desperado, why don't you come to your senses?
—Glenn Frey and Don Henley

Sing sweetly, sadly, gravely.

Beat the big chords from the baby grand.

Bring the full band, and a string quartet for the coda.

Strike a sympathetic note: *Don't your feet get cold?*

Explain what is at risk, all the highs and lows,
even without self-medication
or prescription drugs.

Offer metaphors: Fences. Gates. The sky.

If you sense all this is failing, that your friend remains cold
and lonely, plead and instruct.

Let somebody love you.

Warn him: *Too late. Too late.*

And as the last notes dim and gutter, quiver into absence
and doubt, remember:
it has always been too late.

Take some comfort in the beauty of your song.

Stairway

> *Cheer the slaves, horrify the despots, praise the earth.*
> —Nicholas C. Lindsay

1.
I knew people who wore hooded sweatshirts and work pants,
but they didn't charge into classrooms with an armful of books
and barely manage to tip them onto the desk. I knew people

who earned their living with their hands, but they didn't go on
about dead souls, the mating habits of sparrows, the White Goddess,
Jesus and the joy of closing a couplet, in a single fell swoop.

They didn't bring a box of hand tools to lecture on the Archipelag Gulag.

Have I sinned? Have I not sinned? And what does God get out of it?

2.
I knew people who taught, fine people, their explanations as neat
and orderly as their clothes, as their hair. Then I became one,
almost. The students *like* it when I say small things in clear ways.

But the big things are hard to say clearly. The simplest birdsong
threads itself into the whole shimmering cosmos. The hammer,
the board and the nail all deserve their songs, and the copper mine

and the forest and the city—oh, enough. It's easy to begin, isn't it,
harder to end well. I slip through whole weeks now without
a single strange dream, without saying one thing to surprise myself.

3.
A storm this summer broke the great maple across our driveway,
filled the yard with limbs and leaves. Nothing but to call the crew
with loud saws and big machines, a Bobcat to load the debris,

a boom truck to take down the broken remnants. The rings
were too muddled to count—"many" was all we could agree.
A last machine to grind the stump. The taproot left below to manage

as best it could, hidden and dark, marked only by splinters.
In the time I wasted on that raggy self I could have run
3 rows of pearls around the robe of The Almighty.

4.
That's no place to end. A man is not a tree, not a bird, not
a hooded sweatshirt or a stack of books under the arm. Once,
he told me, he figured out how to swing a circular saw

with the shield off, to carve oak risers for a curving staircase.
I've used those saws myself, cut studs and siding, ripped oak plywood
for bookshelves, everything on the square. But to scrape out

those curves freehand with a roaring, bucking blade? Trickier
than the wildest couplet, the boldest song. Such skill, such labor,
and all done for small wages. Dollars for new boots, for potatoes

and salt. A bumper crop of children and grandchildren.
A long row of books, humming even at rest. And the stairway,
stained and sealed, gleaming in the rich man's house.

Musclewood

Blue Hen to Buttermilk Falls is an easy 20 minutes, even with the roots and creek to slow you down. But it always took an hour with Nelson, who never saw a tree he couldn't explain, a patch of woods that didn't signify.

The Horne-bound tree is a tough kind of Wood, that requires so much paines in riving as is almost incredible, being the best to make bolles and dishes, not subject to cracke or leake.
        -William Wood, New England's Prospect, 1634

My farm boy half, always bent on arriving, sighed when Nelson stopped at a gnarly little tree, its trunk no bigger than my calf, and said, *Oh, this is musclewood.* The settlers tried to use it, he said, but found the wood so tough they mostly gave up, learned to just let it be.

American Hornbeam. Leaves emerge reddish-purple, change to dark green, go yellow to orange-red in fall . . . . The hard wood is used to make golf clubs, tool handles, and mallets.
        -The Morton Arboretum

Touch it, he said, and I wrapped a hand around the trunk,
a comfortable fit. My flesh still remembers the grooved bark,
how it spiraled upward like a long loose-threaded screw.
My hand told me the wood I clutched was dense, pale, stiff
beyond even the oaks and maples, ready to last a long time
between the trail and the creek, easy with a flood now and then.

The Ojibwe people used musclewood as ridgepoles in wigwams. Decoctions of its bark were used in Cherokee, Iroquois, and Delaware medicine to treat painful urination, "diseases peculiar to women," and diarrhea, respectively.
        -The Heartwood Tree Company

Nelson moved west. I'm stuck at home. This absurd,
apocalyptic year creeps slowly toward God knows what.
But the little musclewood is still there, leaning into darkness
and day between the creek and trail, whirling and steady,
pressing out and shedding its new leaves and seeds and flowers,
tough as any tree or trail or creek, any walker stopped
by a curious friend and asked to look, to touch something
native but not common, unassuming, discreet,
of slight human use but entirely at home in its place.
    -for Nelson Strong

Les Bar des PTT

-after Town Meeting by Inge Smith

Four old men on wicker chairs.
They don't hear like they used to,
or see like they used to, or . . . ah,
you get it. They made it here,
they found their tables, they're not
going anywhere soon.

They carry years and decades, wars, women,
delights and disasters, miseries and mysteries
packed snug and tight in their tissues.
Only traces, wordless, in their beards
and shoulders, in their gestures
and the way they lean in to listen.

What do I know? Every face
is a mask, every body,
every gesture hides and reveals.

But this is the age of miracle and wonder
and with only the name Le Bar des PTT
I found the place, a hangout in Aix-en-Provence,
a mid-size but historic city in the south of France,
founded 123 BC by a Roman consul.

There's a Facebook page,
photos of young women
at the outdoor tables,
crowds for soccer games.
You can look it up too.

What does it matter?
The old men would frown and wave
me away if I asked *are you happy?*
But they love each other,
I suddenly believe,
it's in the way they meet each other's gaze,
their regard as weathered and sturdy
as their clothes. One smoking.
One holding a small glass.
Two empty chairs.

Seven Ways into the Pond

> *I say, I'm a sparkle on the waves*
> *as light from a great distance passes*
> *through her wide, moving water.*
>   -Li-Young Lee, "The Invention of the Darling"

1.
The water wishes it could flush all this green shit and shudder its way back to its pure lost youth. The lilies these days, says the water. And don't get me started on the milfoil or the spiny coontail. The purple loosestrife at least has some dignity, and the water willow knows its place, though the roots tickle and sip at me through the muck.

2.
The water has been working on its letters but they keep disappearing. It's hard when you must obey so much, sun and gravity and wind, the clumsy bowl that holds it, even the geese. The earth in its wild spiral journey. Even the clouds leave their mark, and sometimes break down and join, hissing as if in joy or grief.

3.
The water is one and many. Traces slip free to wander the air, drops cling to the kayak the bare-chested man drags up on the beach, a constant trickle noses toward the lordly Hudson and the briny deep.

4.
If the water could remember it would tell astounding stories, dark journeys through stone, glaciers and fogs, cataracts and fens and muddy jungle streams. But the water has no use for stories, does not keep or break promises, does not suffer or elaborate or cry out in quick delight.

5.
What the water understands is simple but not easy. Every moment is a new revelation, every dawn a shining doorway. The Messiah might enter now, or now. The water has no need for a Messiah.

6.
All I know of the water is the side it shows the air. Under that glistening slick might be whole batteries of wisdom, cascades of calculation, glorious psalms and hymns and pop tunes, jazzy mournful improvisations on the brindle of dragonflies, the slow negotiations of the water lilies, the whicker of the cormorant's wings.

7.
For all I know the oldest pickerel and a young painted turtle are conspiring against the otters, plotting revenge. For all I know those three geese splashing just beyond the rope and the No Swimming sign are the appointed guardians, and the water would tell me all its secrets, open the mysteries dark and sacred, heal every bruise and every wound, if only I could call them by their names.

Cornstalks

Every end is a beginning. When everything seems lost,
bald cypress finally plucked clean, empty bottle

tossed in the weeds, muddy water escaping
under the bridge, the deep hum and stir continue.

Time like a cracked door in a great wall,
like a broken shingle that can maybe be glued

back in place, like a letter from a stranger
who somehow found me in his dream.

Like the impossible child reciting Billy Collins
and stacking his dinosaurs at the same time.

Like Allen County's last ring-necked pheasant,
plodding down the waterway bawling for a mate,

trailing its prodigal tail. Like the vast March moon,
distant and puzzled as the face of our lost mother

who has forgotten our number, forgotten where
she left the phone, forgotten who she meant to call.

The Skink Poem

1.
Skink mating strategies are gender-specific, or so Bateson,
Krenz & Sorenson believe. In other ways the five-lined skinks

resemble us as well: they breathe and hear and see,
they eat and defecate, they tend their young.

2.
I doubt I will ever spend my days in the fragrant rotting woods,
my dazzle-blue tail like a flag, skittering through logs and leaves,

over and under, hungry sometimes, sometimes stuffed
on spiders or crickets, termites, snails, fast as anything

but willing in a pinch to ditch my tail and scurry,
with any luck confusing my captor for just long enough.

3.
When there are eggs I mind them, guard them,
as best I can. As for the stories that cats have eaten

our tails and sickened, even died, why would
we skinks desire to spread such odious rumors?

4.
And now the pond reveals how old I am—my head
a yellow-orange bright as an autumn sugar maple.

I cannot smile. Do I wish to smile,
deep in my skinkish self? Do I wish at all?

5.
I have my ways, and they are older than yours,
and I do not need you to blunder into them

and break what you do not understand.
But it may still be that I need you.

Afternoon with Wind, Brown Thrasher, and Dream of Flying

Yes to the brown thrasher, low and speedy, the obstinate sharp
blue jay, the geese like quarrelsome children, birds in the far trees

with their liquid sweet songs beyond my naming, the seagulls white
as hospital sheets curling above the pond as if in pure joy to have found

this small water. When I could fly I was nervous, no, alert,
as is only right when a false move means a messy brutal death.

It was a dream but not "only" a dream. The puzzle of the world
has a million edge pieces, even more all wave or sky, every piece

scattered, battered, jumbled in the drab gray box of explanation,
meaning, words. Any fool can see that the lowest plants green up first.

Twice in my muddy walk I caught myself on berry canes, so the third
time I pulled free from the low snag, then frowned at the neat

new rip in my best old jeans. *Your wallet is showing through your pocket,*
said the TSA man who'd just patted me down, as if he was helping me

somehow. If I flew every night after classes, would I be enlightened
or just exhausted? If these were my woods, how far would I beat

the new growth back from the trails? Today I'm sentimental
as the last goose on the pond, who won't say a thing. I'm earnest

as the brash east wind, dipping and rising, unsatisfied. I'm tender
and smooth as the pond, obeying every lesson of the earth and sky,

keeping all my secrets but two. I'm lucky as the new grass that just
remembered what it has to do, happy as the red-winged blackbird,

deer tracks in the mud, the new rip in my jeans, the barbed wire tag trailing from the fence, the pine trees nodding as the wind directs,

B. in her skirt and leggings and rubber boots. I'm happy as E. with her bare muddy toes, as whoever just rang the new bell to call us back.

Kingfisher, or How Certain Autumn Days Advocate for a Significant Realignment of the Human Project

1.
It's dry everywhere, except where it's flooded. We're all worn out,
clinging by our fingernails to the cliff, waiting for the fall.

Cataclysm or Catharsis was the concert title once in Klaipeda.
A brilliant pianist whose name was almost Genius.

I have it written down. And still things go on, we feed and drink
and breed and sleep. Kingfisher came in hot and low,

speared something small, sped off. Then it's back, chipping,
splashes in again, comes up empty I think. *What do I know, really?*

is the theme, yet again. I know a few things: the harvest is in,
yields mostly good but prices low. I know many Americans

must soon make up their minds, including many who worry me.
Still, M. shopped today, we have chips and fancy cheese, salmon,

mangos. I'll go home soon, wake her from her nap. She'll cook,
I'll clean up, we'll settle in, books and screens, a drink. OK, two.

2.
Most leaves fallen, papery, weathered, crunchy.
Three deer in five minutes walking. Waxing moon,

big and watery in the east. *Is that true,* I keep asking,
a healthy question I think but time-consuming.

It's chill and windy and I'm still hacking wads
of sputum but it's good to be out. Not a single tree

seems worried or elated about anything
Americans have done or not done lately.

This may be their mistake, but their sources
provide only limited information. The moon

is even less concerned. We look at her way more
than she looks at us, though she'll notice

if the lights go off. What do I know. Right?
What I know is not the problem, it's how

damn little I can do about anything. I barely try anyway.
Write poems. Walk around in the tattered woods.

And then some new photos on the family chat, and
I laugh and text back quickly, and a red-tail

circles over and away to the north and at last
my ridiculous self-pity lifts. Here I am, alone

in the woods, safe and chilly in the late golden sun,
and another white-tail startles and sprints hard

across the plowed field, tail high, as if she thinks
I'm going to chase her with my old legs.

Did she know I will steal her wild, floating image,
carry her ghost home to light so gently on this page,

to leap and leap across its furrows and away?

Reports from an Interior Province

1. Some December

It all begins when everything seems dead,
bald cypress finally plucked clean, dirty paper

tossed in the weeds, muddy water rushing
toward the ocean. Time like a locked door,

like a crumbled sidewalk, like an old friend
vanished halfway through the chorus.

The broken stalks exhausted in the fields,
barely breathing, waiting for the test results,

sick to their hollow bones. The March moon,
distant and stony and not looking down

upon us, not looking anywhere at all.

2. The Great Pure Dazzle

Some days the light is just too much, blasting the tender
new leaves of the linden, even here where not much attention

gets paid. Being ignored is privilege, as it's taken me years
to understand. I was a straight white country kid

with plenty to eat and pretty good parents and only
the prospects of nuclear annihilation, an eternity

of fiery torment, and stochastic bullying to trouble my nights.
Some mornings the light was too much, winter days

with the snow a great pure dazzle. Some days I hid my eyes.
Some days I stared too long at the girls as they blossomed

and preened, preened and blossomed, all of us
baffled by their new powers. I learned to sweat,

to run hard one way, turn, lean and wait for the whistle
and run hard back. Some days I got home after dark,

empty as a new wineskin, sore and weary, still all
the chores to do before we could crowd around the table.

3. The New Knee

We judge our neighbors by how well
they clear their walks and driveways,
with minor allowances for those
who live on corner lots, or alone.

B. raps at us from his upstairs window,
waves wildly. We wave back, pleased,
we used to meet on Wednesday nights
at the pub downtown, walk home
happy and a little tipsy. How long
since we actually talked?

We grumble across the snow pack,
your new knee tender and stiff,
then choose the street, mostly clear,
empty unless the school kids
and teachers are coming or going.

Don't walk on loose dirt, E. taught me
long ago, it makes it way harder to

shovel it back when you're done.
It's true of snow too, everybody
knows, way better to shovel
when it's fresh. Not much to do
after you drive it flat and icy
but wait for a thaw.

4. Every Day of February 2021

The forecast is cold, then snow, then colder. M.'s knee
is better every day, a little, she's even done the basement stairs

although she grumbles. And now even the cardinals
have gone dark across their backs and wings. I've tromped

a sort of path to the feeders but it's lumpy and treacherous
as I clamber around the pile at the end of the driveway.

The birds love safflower seed, empty our biggest feeder
in half a day, scatter most of it on the ground where the doves

and squirrels and finches mingle to peck and nibble.
The sparrows in their dozens flock in and out, skittish,

never at rest for long, I wonder how they don't burn
more energy than they can eat. I'm more or less

the same, not in motion but in mind, flitting here
and there, never at rest for long enough to rest.

Instructions for Surviving the Eclipse, the Merger, and the Flood
—A Cento

Don't stare at the sun.

The Bluffton Police asked that we remind you to please avoid the flood waters for your safety. The water is not safe for swimming. Do not go swimming, or rafting or attempt to float down the Riley.

Nor trivial Loss, nor trivial Gain despise;
Molehills, if often heap'd, to Mountains rise.

THROUGHOUT THE ALIGNMENT, EACH UNIVERSITY'S STRONG ROOTS AS AN INSTITUTION OF HIGHER LEARNING GROUNDED IN CHRISTIAN FAITH AND COMMITTED TO ACADEMIC EXCELLENCE WILL BE HONORED.

Don't write about / what is happening in
the world, / the missing child / and the
human remains . . .

Campus is closed to the public on April 8 for the solar eclipse. No classes or athletic practices will take place and doors to all buildings will be locked. Do not allow non-university people into buildings or residence halls.

This is what you shall do; Love the earth and sun and the animals, despise riches, give alms to every one that asks, stand up for the stupid and crazy, devote your income and labor to others, hate tyrants, argue not concerning God . . .

If anything but the sun shows through the eclipse glasses, they're no good.

SPLIT A PIECE OF WOOD; I AM THERE. LIFT UP THE STONE, AND YOU WILL FIND ME THERE.

... re-examine all you have been told at school or church or in any book, dismiss whatever insults your own soul ...

Do not slaughter your friends and neighbors with a stone knife to propitiate the gods.

... and your very flesh shall be a great poem ...

Faculty should not be on campus, and friends/family of faculty, staff and students are not permitted on campus.

A poem should be equal to. / Not true.

During totality you can take off your eclipse glasses. Then put them back on.

The Poet Resists His Own Instructions
at the Nature Preserve

There's a big late-afternoon moon, the trails are muddy, and people are yelling *Fuck you* across the pond. They found something. It's a deal. The geese waddled up the steep bank already, as if they know something.

I don't know much, and also way too much. Soon the *fuck you* women pass behind me, young, both wearing thin black sweaters, no coats. They start yelling again. Someone by the dock yells back. Who *are* they?

Should I yell at them for yelling? The prompt I gave my students said to put famous people in their poems, not strangers yelling *fuck you*. The geese have their own loud problems. The moon doesn't seem to care.

A thin cloud like a Chinese character written on wet paper shrouds it, drifting into one arcane new ideogram after another. Two cardinals call back and forth. Most days I'm happier out here than with people,

who make it so hard to be both gentle and right, to say anything simple. *Imitate Socrates and Jesus,* said Ben Franklin. The Decembrists and Lin-Manuel Miranda wrote a wild song about him: *Do you know*

who the fuck I am? Ben demands, over and over. It got cut from *Hamilton*. Earlier Peter Elbow noted that teachers must be infinitely supportive and infinitely challenging. Not easy, he admitted. He also mentioned

Jesus and Socrates. We know how things turned out for them. Geese are geese, after all, and the moon is the moon, and after seeking to add humility to his list of personal virtues, Ben claimed only

that he'd gotten pretty good at *appearing* humble. Long ago I wrote a whole essay on humility and Mennonites, said it was a good idea. Several women pointed out that for them, humility mainly meant

knuckling under to some asshole. This partly changed my mind,
as often happens after I partly study things I partly understand.
By now the woman have met up and quit yelling, but the geese started up

again, and I swear they're hollering *Fuck you* to each other, and it escalates
until two of them take loudly off and fly right over me. And despite
all my efforts to resist my own instructions, Ben and the Decembrists

are here on the page. And the trails and my shoes and my heart are all
muddy with the good brown rich sauce of this messy fucking world.

Seven Ways of Looking at Raspberries

1.
Between the compost pile
and the birdfeeders
there are only the raspberries.

2.
Except for the asparagus,
head high and prickly.
And the vines, volunteer mulberries
and redbuds and maples.
And the thistles. And the ground ivy.

3.
A gardener and his raspberries
are not one.
A gardener and his raspberries and asparagus
and innumerable uncultivated flora and fauna
are one.

4.
The Japanese beetles
suckle the sweet red juice of raspberries
and mate ecstatically among the leaves.

5.
In the dark earth
raspberry runners nuzzle
and murmur all winter.

6.
Every good boy
deserves raspberries
eaten straight from the canes.

7.
At the rate of nine inches a year
the raspberries are marching.

8.
Once there were seven raspberry canes
dug from the friendly preacher's back yard,
carried home in a black plastic bag.

9.
The plum trees behind the raspberries
were released from their earthly bonds
decades ago.

10.
In the same humid morning
an earnest gardener can pick raspberries
and pull thistles
with fair results.

11.
Raspberries do not count,
but they multiply.

12.
There are more than seven ways
of looking at raspberries.

Wednesday at the Pond

1.
What is it with the geese? A wild town meeting?
A fight over mates, or food? Are the zealots

among them demanding The Gays and The Sluts
be drowned or strangled in the strong names of Jesus

and the Few Holy Verses? They calm down, a little.

2.
Something told me to walk slow today, while it's warm
and calm. Half the pond is skinned with brittle ice.

The geese are way over on the island, or in the open water.
They ignore me without even deciding to.

3.
Behind me the children are home from school,
calling to each other house to house,

meeting in their muddy yards.

5.
Sperm whales sleep vertically, near the surface,
prefer at least two miles of water below.

They use clicks to hunt and signal—the strongest
bursts of sound made by anything alive.

When a mother dives, leaving the baby behind,
an aunt or grandmother stays nearby.

6.
A milkweed pod on the shoreline has burst open,
seeds still clinging, Like any paranoid

or mystic I can't help but believe
the things I encounter all connect

though the threads are hard to see. White fluff
waves in the faint breeze, not yet free.

7.
Four more geese, no, six, and when they settle
on the ice they break right through. A little rest

and they flap off to join the others, leaving
open traces that could almost be wounds,

if the pond were a gigantic animal.

8.
The pond is not an animal. I am trying to learn
a few small things, to get them right.

I am sure to run out of time. I am only sure
the world opens in many places,

and not all of them are wounds.

Threshold Signal

> *—A received radio signal (or radar echo) with power just above the noise level of the receiver.*
> —Meteorological Glossary

God is always sick with love, we learned, and Vladimir was his apt
and eager pupil, though his pain threshold was disappointing.

Yet as we plunged into the darkness, we found ourselves
running short of words. All our beautiful ideas failed as arguments.

God was none of the things we could say, even after we rejected
the commonplace that women were misbegotten males,

even after we pushed Aristotle into the dust bin. *Being cannot suffer
at all,* Caputo proclaimed, *cannot suffer oblivion or disaster.*

All well and good, we replied, *And yet a displaced threshold may be used
for takeoff but never for landing.* We sweated every approach and vector.

We wanted to discover the strongest possible grammar.
We knew all points of entry may also be points of departure.

We knew the signal must be strong enough to clear the noise.
In the end we rediscovered the old books, cut the zip ties,

gave the prisoners water and energy bars. *A big misunderstanding,*
we said, *swear to God.* But he had already turned the corner.

Implicit Bias in the Wilds of Allen County

Only a few of us ever need to whistle Vivaldi to reassure
the nervous suburbanites. Some of us answer "tired old prof"

when asked our true identity, or "Captain Marvel wannabe."
Nobody says "mere white guy," and this goes unremarked.

Not in my weirdest dreams did I ever think that Jesus
looked like me. I failed the Implicit Association Test,

but doesn't everybody? I plead to numerous implicit biases:
geese are stupid, cats are arrogant. Don't get me started

on the Patriots. But it's true: when I went walkabout
nobody jumped me from behind, nobody rolled up and

hit the siren. I confess: mostly I don't have a clue.
I mocked those two smooth couples in the convertible,

but they had lost it all to the great storm, they were driving
the ruins in shock and heartache, checking their phones

for texts from friends who might be dead. Who knew?

Clay into Birds

Mammoth gatherings are happening elsewhere.
But we are here, where we can be counseled
to lean toward whatsoever things are funny,
small, astonishing, oblique. Once the alphabet
was magic, once the leaves spoke a language
the wise heard behind their eyes.

Once a strange hand fisted clay into birds,
and images slipped from one mind to another
like breath, like wind, like electrons
slipping inside the airy hearts of protons
and out again, shaking out their fur.

Once there was twice as much time,
time enough for singing and hunting,
time for the rough mysticism of
a well-used broom, a pitchfork,
and trysts in the secret grottos too.

And then there was nothing but rain,
nothing but desire for a well-lit room
and creatures resembling ourselves.

We can never hear what others mean,
exactly, and yet we go on, daily
launching sounds into the distances
like spider silk, like swaying bridges,
like the word that is always a gift,
always magical yet not magic,
patient as the foggy membranes
that will someday be a star.

—for Obi Martin

Little Bridges

God is in the space at the hub of the wheel,
but God is not only there.

I think the spokes are like the little bridges
we have built into God's domain,

spun of almost nothing so they float,
thinner than thought, among canyons

and mountains, oceans and creatures,
worlds and stars and galaxies without bound.

Those who feel their way along these bridges
cannot go very far, and once they have tried

they can never come all the way back.
But they do not seem to mind.

Sunday Morning at River Ridge Mansion

In praise or lamentation, peace or desperation,
Any way I do, I come into the presence of the Lord.
        -Dave Carter and Tracy Grammer, "Any Way I Do"

When I look out my window, still rubbing my eyes, a young woman in a long brown dress and white covering is gazing into the valley, taking pictures with her phone. She dances away, swaying to a music I can't hear.

From downstairs, stray notes settle into "Great Is Thy Faithfulness," played slowly, with many runs and flourishes. It's probably Hope or Charity, two young sisters who brought a full-size harp along. Last night they did a little concert, classical pieces, dolled up in fancy period dresses they made themselves. One played harp, one the harpsichord. I'm not sure which sister is which, but both play beautifully, and are beautiful. Usually they dress plain, but not *that* plain.

Mist for the second straight morning. Under the heavy columns of the shelter the little fountain burbles. Children's voices, happy for now. A big flight of geese headed south, a small one going west.

This little band of poets and writers in plain dress, gathered in the vast old mansion to scheme and talk and laugh and listen, let me join them despite my worldly ways. They ask where I'm from, tell me bits of their stories. Half seem to have the last name Martin, but all the Martins insist they are barely related to all the other Martins.

News comes to us through the air, as the trees share their needs and desires through the earth. Twenty dead in El Paso, more dead in Dayton. Torrents of lost ice pour liquid, still cold, from Greenland into the sea.

Even the highest branch is not separate or alone. The yellow bird on the highest branch is not separate or alone.

The brown-eyed woman rocking on the swing greeted me and then was quiet. We sat together and apart under the big stone shelter, content.

As the mist burns away, sun lights the high shoulders of the trees. Something golden gleams like a tiny sun among the branches.

Others are measuring coffee into a machine, breaking eggs and stirring them together, practicing for the service, watching over their scrambling children, climbing through the gears on the hilly highway.

This is not paradise. But what is it then, and what then shall we do?

We walked uphill to the little white chapel, paneled inside with dark-stained plywood. We sang a cappella in four parts, old songs from well-worn Methodist hymnals. A man read some verses from Tagore, another some scripture. The preacher told us, without harshness or anger, that God didn't choose his people because they were worthy, but just because, the way a man chooses a woman, or a woman chooses a man.

God demands to be loved, he said, for similar reasons, and left us to rest in that.

I hoped the bird might be a yellow warbler but likely it was a goldfinch, lovely but common, kin to those that flit like stray sparks from the ditches back home.

The tiny sun was no such thing—only a yellow leaf, a trick of the light, a brilliant speck among the common green.

Praise or lamentation? Peace or desperation? I hope no one will mistake these words for explanation. I hope no one will load a gun and empty it at anyone, today at least. I know how little my hope means, how hard it is to lever the world off its heavy course. Demands are less difficult than obedience. A crying child cannot always be consoled, no matter how patient its mother, how gentle its father, no matter how kind.

The Guy with the Pumpkin on His Head

It's cut like a helmet, this small pumpkin.
It seems to fit him well enough.
He has a black cap underneath.
Everybody on his dorm floor got a pumpkin, he explains, to carve.
It seems to fit you, I say.
It hurts, he says.
You could take it off, I say. *We wouldn't think less of you.*

G. gives him her sly side-eye, saying nothing.
Her poems are full of half-spoken sorrow.
She lights up at rare intervals, grins like she understands everything,
then her mask comes down like an overhead door.

The others are quiet. For once nobody's on their phone.
It occurs to me that we ought to get started.
He sits there next to G., the pumpkin on his head.
He's done about 7% of the work for my class.
I made a promise, he says. *I promised I'd wear it all day.*

Sunset Hill, Father's Day

Exercise, observation and contemplation are not mutually exclusive
but may be orthogonal to each other, if I understand that word

a-right. I'm trying to walk fast and notice everything and slip
into the poet-trance all at once. Sun and breeze after the night's rain.

I won't get far today because somehow I've become patriarch of the group,
and even slipping off for half an hour seems a betrayal. But it's all right,

I'm out, it's warm but not sweltering, I can give up a few drops
of blood where blackberry thorns caught a wrist. That might be a tick

on my sock, but my legs seem uninvaded. Traffic and birdsong,
half-burnt embers in the fire ring. Nodding grasses with old words

to say. The valley spreading westward, definite but concealing
almost everything, as happens in these hills, as happens.

None of this is permanent, but some things are durable.
If the rocks remember anything it won't be me, passing sudden

as a cloud-shadow, heading back to hug my grandsons
large and small as they pile into their car seats, weary and happy,

sweaty from their play, as my sons and their wives speak softly
to them, take their own seats and back out, crunch the gravel lane

to the blacktop, to the highway that will smooth the boys home
as they grumble a little, as they nod, as they fade into easy dreams.

Pura Vida at Tambor Beach

1.
I woke early again, almost made it out
for sunrise. At the beach all is golden

and blue, a few people strolling or sitting,
the Coast Guard ship anchored half a mile out

like a sentinel, a specter, a heavy ghost.
Somebody lost her phone and is stalking

like a shorebird whose nest is threatened.
Somebody's arms are flung high and wide

to greet the sun. Somebody left a full cup
of beer and three empties in the sand.

A white-winged dove keeps asking
the same question. Nobody answers

except the kingbird and the rose-throated
becard, each in its own tongue. The path

to the sun is a brilliant broken dazzle
like wine run over from a goblet.

A red and brown squirrel climbs my tree,
gives me the eye and sees I have nothing

for him. Two swimmers out beyond where
the waves break, two cormorants so low

they seem to skip off the water,
two lovely women taking each other's

photo, arms wide for the new day.
They meet their friends, stand in a ring

at the water's edge, and because I can't hear
what they're saying I am sure it is holy.

2.
Here in the land of *pura vida* it seems
lucky to wake early. Still cool at six,

the macaws still quiet. The pretty women
don't care who looks at them from far away.

The girl on the boat last night was only twelve.
She stood tall as we left, gripping the frame

above her, black curls bouncing with the waves.
She helped her uncle carry the heavy cooler

up on the beach and then sat back away from us,
got out her phone, refused a drink. Soon a boy

from another boat was sitting with her,
holding a heavy stick, lifting and dropping

it in the sand. When we docked she helped us
cross from the boat, she reached out

her slender hand and I held it for a moment.

3.
It was harder than I thought to put on the mask
and slide into the dark water. I bit down

on the mouthpiece, wondering whose teeth,
whose lips, had been there before mine.

Then I waved my hands like a curious child
and a swirl of flashes filled the water, bright

as tiny suns, as welding sparks, again, again,
the small lives flared and winked away as if

I'd been given one small but real magical power.
I was clumsy in the water, fearful I would lose

the boat somehow. Keeping her eyes on me,
my wife stumbled in the boat, leaned hard

on a rail and bent the glasses I'd left her to hold.

4.
I've been bending them back slowly, this way
and that, fearful I'll snap the thin frames.

So far they've held. So far it seems clear:
I will never see quite the same way again.

Phantom #9

> *"Americans need to think more about death."*
> —Somebody on the internet

1.
Chilly day, just enough sun to melt
the top inch of grass, soften the trail
enough to tear at a sudden turn,
even a firm landing. The passage

of deer and even rabbits still
inscribed in the grass and moss,
as if I suddenly awoke to them.

2.
So much I miss. What words
for a thousand shades of brown,
for the way each leaf has found
to a temporary rest?

3.
Seemed I was walking
for a long time. Then before me

small leaves on the path
were like chimes

in the low light
like spilt coins

like torn-up programs
from last year's game

like glittering promises
from the other side

Looking for the Path

1.
The Omega Institute provides a map that shows
the Hill House trail starting just past Nirvana House

and leading up to the Omega Trail and then to The Path.
So I turned left, but the trail petered out between

two white cabins. So I walked on and took the next left
and there a little way up the hill I found Yearning Pond,

a glimmery body lined in stone. It bears a clear sign,
but the falling water had only one small thing to say.

2.
So I went on up the hill and found Sanctuary
with all its low red brick and took off my shoes

as the sign asked and inside were many mats
and chairs and three people sitting very quietly

while the AC whooshed like the last whirr
of some great non-calamity, as if the universe

had begun with the clapping of one giant hand.

3.
And my research question was not made clear,
nor was my structure illuminated. And still I had

no idea how to argue anything except beauty
and sorrow and music. So I sat on a bench in the back

and hoped to disturb no one, and I studied
the grand hard sweeping stones that line

the north wall and the east wall of Sanctuary.
The stones also had only one word to say,

a long hard word, and I could not speak or write it
so I stored it with all the hard and quiet things I keep

in a little chamber that is bigger on the inside.

Purple

Years ago I learned not to fight every battle,
not to dive into black holes or drive through

floodwaters, not to pin my hopes on any group
larger than seven. I learned that I could wear

my jeans to school or church, even with grass stains
on the knees, and no one but my wife would say a word.

Some Saturdays I broke an extra egg into the shaker,
made the omelet with red pepper, onions, mushrooms,

sharp cheddar, bleu cheese, and we ate every bite.
Everybody seems to love my old purple shirt,

which has never once been ironed, and has faded
so well that even its wrinkles are beautiful.

One afternoon on the island I snuck down
the private road to the private beach where the flour-

white shells lay in drifts, fluffy and sharp.
I snuck back unchallenged and felt like Robin Hood,

though I had nothing to give to the poor or anyone
except a few shards I dumped out of my shoes.

When they told us the new slogan was *The Power
of Purple,* I didn't even groan. I told my grown-up kids,

and they groaned for me. Some sweaty nights
I think I should have fought at least one great battle.

When I noticed the smoke I should have run
for the bucket, I should have pulled the alarm,

I should have tried to save the children. Was it
a dream? I took to the streets now and then,

but I never even got myself arrested. And now
my purple shirt hangs in the closet

for months on end before I think to pull it out.
Once I put it on and walked into the woods

with Nelson and some others and he knelt and touched
the wild soap bush, named the muscle wood,

the tulip tree, the grand red oak, the understory
stripped by deer. He spoke of the lacy net of things,

its intricate shining, its hidden nodes, how it
glowed and trembled and bled and burned,

and to be there with him was like walking in the garden
on the first day after all things found their names.

INQUIRIES

(1992)

Seek and learn to recognize who and what,
in the midst of the inferno, are not inferno,
then make them endure, give them space.

-Italo Calvino, *Invisible Cities*

Chainsaw Inquiries

What do chainsaws love?

> Lumber, dust. Live wood pulled down
> by the dying. Sun on last year's leaves.

Do chainsaws share a hidden fear?

> Rocks. Nails. A few, older, fear
> their appetites, and that what they chew
> does not nourish them.

If chainsaws dream, of what?

> Of hands that never tire, tanks
> that never empty. Forests
> rising quick as grass. A heaven
> where silence never falls.

Do chainsaws share a hidden grief?

> They cannot hold what they eat,
> cannot keep what they kill.
> They cannot feed themselves.

Inquiries into the Technology of Hell and Certain Rumors Recently Circulating

> "The snowball arrives in hell every morning at 7."
> —Jack Spicer

And so they come up on us after we thought
we were free, better or not, after we thought
we had almost settled things. And they say:
We don't expect sympathy. We don't expect
trust, faith, any of that, we know how long
we made our gestures and you yawned, as bored
and unpersuaded as we were ourselves, needing
a new sign. You won't believe it. But here
it is anyway, the truth being a wall sometimes
for comfort and regret, some sort of answer.

It happened in hell, they say. That place.
You don't have to believe. But that day
it happened that a little boy was up
and roaming the great halls. Despite
the old sermons they were dim and almost
cool those mornings, waiting for the bell
to bring the fires back, the monotonous,
earnest screams. And there it was, you know,
they said, don't ask us why or how, it was,
white and eerie in that world of red
and black, steaming just a little, ready.

The technology of hell was barely medieval,
let along postmodern. Enormous yellow pipes
and hoppers, dirty yellow flames, everything
clogged and filthy with centuries when security
had never been a problem. So there was the little
night burn in an alcove, not even fenced off.
So there was the ball in the child's hands,

dripping, so cold. Why not? He was still young,
somehow. He remembered the year after Kennedy
died, how three boys with a bucket found the flame
on the grave that was advertised as eternal.
Play is a wild teacher. Of course he panicked
when the flames hissed and died. No matter.
In hell the gas had no metaphors or mercaptans:
it slipped into low places, trying to think,
to remember. Who could have thought.

And so the staff awoke cold and confused,
and so hours passed as they blundered
through the blueprints, and so some ordinary
devil lit the match.
                        And so.
A snowball, a child, a match, and now
we come to see you, holding all this
like sacks of stale groceries, inventing
the questions you ought to ask: *Is it true
that the maps are useless? That all
the old rooms are ash and splinters?
What is it that the wild ones taste
in the dust that settles from the hot wind?*

We look at the floor, think of the children,
harrumph. We hint that we gave at the office,.
And so they say: Fine. Don't worry. We will be
in the good room, plotting our course, laying
our claims, sorting our stories. We do not
insist you take this one as true. We do not
require or forbid you to gather at the river,
or kneel in the evening, or dust your shelves.
When you want to hear, we will tell you again.

Inquiries into the Technology of Beauty
    (after Apollinaire)

I am going to explode. I have been instructed.
I have read Apollinaire in the original
and the 1980 University of California translation.
I have heard 'the thunder of the guns accomplishing
the terrible love of nations' and have seen
the shells bursting like flowers, like breasts,
I have learned that we 'must still consider Beauty
the one thing on earth which is never evil.'
I will be beautiful when I explode.

        *

Remember the hole in the medicine cabinet,
the one you've casually stuffed
with razor blades all these years? How often
have you remembered them down there in the dark,
nudging together, rusting, sharpening
their secret grudges? They are eager
to show how deep they still can cut.
Their silvery arcs will glimmer, gay
as light flung by the dawn's fountain.

        *

I don't need to explode. Spinning from beauty
are a thousand subtle strands. I can make you think only
of the delicate petals of prepubescent girls
for the rest of your life. You will steer
all conversations toward them, scrawl endless
mutant sonnets and rondels in their praise.
Your mother will move to Nevada in disgust.
Your best friends will pool their reputation
to buy plastic explosive for your last birthday,
and be acquitted to general rejoicing.

        *

I don't want to explode. Instead
I will make you love me, and be the lover
of your father's direst fears. I won't show up
when you have the candles out and
the *coq au vin* simmering. I will call
two days later, neither penitent nor afraid.
I will write intricate, exhausting poems
from the front, detailing my suffering
and my vision of your black hair, your breasts,
sustaining me through the fire flowers
of flashing sleet. You will find the same poems
in the drawer of the redhaired nurse.

                    *

How war has nourished the art of invisibility.
The bomblets may even now be in your lawn.
Cunningly crafted of unsniffable plastic,
they will leap waist high like startled rabbits,
letting you glimpse their gorgeous symmetry.
The pellets tunnel flesh like wasps
through deadfall pears. Think of your children
as they flop and scream, think what delicate lines
the beauty of uncertainty will etch
between your brows. Don't be sorry.

                    *

Think of the wonder of the white missiles
arguing gravity into consent. Think of the beauty
of their smooth arc, classical, serene.
Think of the elegant use of space,
the fine metals crafted to silken tolerances,
the chips solving thousands of problems
at once and all gracefully, all beautifully,
all for a love that will spend the world
to bring 'the terrible love of nations'
to you, to you, to you.

Inquiry into the Discovery of the City
 into Which the Saints Have Been Said
 to Go, Marching

> *Heaven is dead.*
> —Mallarmé

Don't ask how we did it. Call it fate or harmony
or tax dollars at work, the grasping that exceeds
our reach. Partly instrumental, partly mystic,
but we found it. And three days from the border,
on a wide, deserted, unworn road, the city.
The old black book had it right: fifteen hundred miles
on a side, the walls of seamless, dark green quartz,
the twelve pearl gates, the graceful buildings.
All that had changed was that everyone was gone.

We wandered far into the realm, across all sorts
of terrain, and found no other sign. The roads
all lead to the city, but moving out turn oddly vague
and hard to follow. There were a few early moments
when our instruments seemed to pick up haunting, near-
familiar songs, when we found ourselves among mysteries.
Like most mysteries, they refused to come clean.

The press has floated many schemes for the place,
but all of them founder on logistics and supply:
the distances are huge, travel hard in the dark
and full moons. And while the city is great and glorious
it lacks sewers, plumbing, stairways, public transport.
Some buildings are hollow, windowless husks, others filled
with tangles of shelves and pillars. No hospitals,
single-family homes, kitchens, parking lots.

And yet despite all we say they keep coming,
some with nothing but their hands, others lugging
pack frames full of nylon and freeze-dried food.
Bright tents dot the hillsides, and campstoves
glow and hiss at all hours. The climate is mild,
of course, and trees near the river bear fruit.
A pale sort of fungus can be gathered and eaten
though it won't keep. Nothing can be cultivated.

Still, if the place has defeated our usual interests,
no one has given up or died. The tourists avoid
the planned attractions and refuse to leave
when their money is gone. They walk the streets
wearing robes they bring or make somehow, talk
endlessly about truth and God and beauty. They sit
in circles picking banjos and dulcimers, singing
old gospel songs. They act for all the world
as if they mean to stay forever.

Inquiry into What One Can Do
with a Rented Jackhammer

It is almost fun, aside from the noise
which is stereotypically thunderous
and my general irritation at having
to mess around at all with this
rooting up footings through doorways
laid wrong due to the slovenly,
arrogant and slapdash work habits
of these overpriced big-city trades
who refuse to accept any responsibility
except to come late, throw together something
vaguely resembling the blueprints,
and contribute to the velocity
of currency circulation in the province
by being paid the instant they're
almost done. But never mind,
never mind, after a month when the framers
cunningly avoided showing up at all
my father-in-law is glad for anything
that happens. And here in the basement
with the rented electric jackhammer between
my legs things are definitely happening,
I have as big, noisy and irresistible a weapon
as any irritable pacifist could want.
The concrete is stubborn, young and strong,
giving up only puffs of dust at first,
but like a stupid but persistent teacher
the jackhammer makes the smallest flaws
mean something. Chunks of fresh rubble
give up one by one, and what was firm
and smooth and wrong gets carried up
and dumped along the foundation. We challenge
each other politely for the chance to hammer,

and before we know it's done and ready
for tomorrow's labor and mistakes.
We look over and approve, box the hammer up,
and leave humming with temporary power.

Inquiry into the Nature of Beauty,
or the Tale of the King of the Cats

A man went on a journey to a mud-plump creek,
a man went with a weight upon him
he had no excuse or explanation for,
a man went stiff and somber
through a brilliant June day
and insects buzzed him till his ears
were red from his own boxing
and he studied the layers of trees and shadows
the muddy creek held up for anybody
and he half guessed at the names of trees,
maple, elm, sycamore.
And he remembered the story
of the great red oak someone chopped
and abandoned, how it was found
the next day, leaves crisping,
no explanation or excuse. And he thought
of the tale of the house cat who overheard
the odd story, "Tell Dimble that Dumble
is dead!" and spoke once:
"Then I'm the King of the Cats!"
and was gone up the chimney.
Hints, stories slippery as neutrinos,
sliding into and through us, leaving
changes we strain to notice:
Go, go, go, said Eliot's bird.
We crave only reality, said Thoreau.
We live, said the man, in the craving
that will kill us. The hard trunks
and the supple branches and the leaves moved
together, using all the light they had.
In one bank's shadow, trees and sky
and clouds laid their colors down

full and gentle on water only a crawdad
could love. The man thought: I am sad
because I meant to write today, and now
I have. Because of the cats. Because
beauty is not truth, or justice, or love.
Because it is something to love.

Inquiry into Gifts, or the Indigo Bunting

After hearing on the radio news
of the beautiful indigo bunting,
of its luminous blue-green splendor
that is visible only with the sun
at your back, I see one that very night
standing calmly on the lawn of a dream.
It knows full well how strange and rare
it is, knows it may live its days out
before anyone sees. As though
the world was made not to be noticed,
as though God had some job for us
beside seeing, as though eyes were given
for making the right turns and keeping
the rows straight. This is romantic,
isn't it? What can I say.
Some dumb gritty pressure,
habit or ideology, is warping me
toward a cautionary space where the birds
are all robins and grackles, beautiful
not even to each other, noisy
and jealous of their turf,
sure that if there is a God
he has done nothing for them lately.
I hear a strange bird call and
look toward the sun and see
a dark shadow, a figure that shakes
itself off to a further branch
before it even hears me looking,
to remind me that what is given in dreams
should not be expected again.

Flatlands

(1995)

Where I Live

> *For the families of nine other area residents, the day [of the 1965 Palm Sunday tornado] was a most serious tragedy. . . . As was reported then, Mrs. Arnold died later at Bluffton Community Hospital. The others were buried in their homes or thrown into the fields.*
> *Their names remain as the saddest of reminders.*
> —*The Bluffton News*, April 12, 1990

In my town it's too boring for buggies, except on parade days.
There is however a car with one orange and three blue fenders,
there are men slamming lids on their pickups and turning
toward the kitchen. And the paper lies all over town,
on tables and toilets, the young editor's weird dirge
front and center. Did you think about it? Did you see
the bodies buried in the basements and forgotten,
thrown into the fields like orange peels or mice?

Where I live we are trying to render our losses, but the work
is slow. We say nothing for years and then go loud
and clumsy as the men on state hourly rates who leveled
a mile of thickets for the new bike path. Today, snow fell
at ten on the bright grass and was gone by one.
I don't know how to render much so I keep going,
over sidewalks cracked by frost and thaw until they shift
and rumble as I plod across them, past a little tree
bearing plastic eggs for Jesus, asking who are these people,
what sort of poem are they writing, where do I live.

> *It's been twenty-five years and the signs
> have all rusted. We had almost managed
> to forget the bodies thrown into the fields.*
>
> *We're sorry, we did not know who was
> in charge, we wanted only to put splinters
> and the smell of broken stone behind us.*

*We don't know where to find them now, or what
to offer. So we put them into bold print
in the paper, on the front page in a black box,*

*twenty-five years buried in their homes,
thrown into the fields. We dream them
all over again, flat in the corn*

*like feed sacks fallen from the truck.
We hear the wind again, tugging us all
toward some laughter, some work to do.*

Knowing the Father

It's a good day for sweat to find and coat
my glasses in big smeary salty drops that
I puzzle how to remove without leaving a film
sticky and implacable as the religion
of my childhood, the prayers that demanded
a surrender so ultimate that even as I tried
I could never quite grasp it as possible,
or connect to the way the eggs still had
to be gathered the next day, the yellow
plastic-coated wire basket to be filled
gingerly as I went from coop to coop, shooing
the stupid hens aside, batting at the ones
who'd peck if you didn't slap them away.

I thought I should feel different, the day after,
but if I did it was only in my testing
how it felt, my puzzling: Is this right?
Am I saved? What is it shuffling in
the cobs with me, breathing chicken dirt?
I already knew, somehow: I wanted
a dark, bold sign. I didn't deserve it.
I would have to keep looking.

When the eggs were in the cooler
and supper done I could sometimes
wheedle my father into playing catch.
His glove was dark and old, his fingers
thick from the fields. He threw hard
and left handed. People in town
still talked about how good he'd been,
how he started as a freshman.
Now he was thirty, and that was over.
The ball went back and forth until
we lost it in the dusk, and then
he gathered me under his hard left arm,
and we found the door together.

Squirrels

Everything leaks. The drains leak, the faucets leak, the shower leaks, the hose to the dishwasher which I spent an hour last night putting a new end on still leaks, and the plywood under the sink is soggy and warping. The house leaks at the foundation where the mice get in, around the chimney where the squirrels get in, and after multiple efforts and pieces of sheet metal I'm still not sure of anything. The roof leaks, not much, just a little around the dormers, and the paint in the boys' room is bubbled and the plaster is soft and crumbly where the water's run in, not much water, just a cup or two here, a few tablespoons there, dribbles and bits. The right front car tire won't hold air or lose it fast enough that I just have to do something, and so every week I try to get to the gas station and pump it up and am always tempted to put forty pounds in it so it'll be longer till the next time, and then I figure it'll just leak faster if it has more pressure so I don't.

I'm halfway convinced that all these things are just what I deserve for my general vagueness and laziness, my habit of drifting off to something else nine-tenths of the way through any particular project. But it's more than that, it's why ocean liners have pumps, why basements do, why this human world is filled with drains and valves and sealants, gunk and foil and visqueen, instruments and mixtures and layers. It's far beyond cliche, these clumsy efforts to keep things sealed against the weary haulings of gravity, the wobbly yearning of the whole breathing world toward chaos and the depths.

The squirrel chewed around my first two patches, once from the inside, once from out. I plant the ladder in the mud and head back up. The wood's barely solid anywhere nearby, but I start bending tin to fit anyway. Even all this talk is only more leakage, mere distraction, the literary world seeping in drop by drop in its sinister way, if I'm not careful instead of nailing this tin I'll find myself quoting Camus or some other dead Frenchman, tipping out over that abyss as I can feel the ladder start to slide in the mud, steady, steady, it leans and leans but it's bound to stop soon if I hold my breath and think light thoughts, steady, if not I can ride it down slowly, surely, the sweat on my palms is a sign I'm ready for anything, slowly I take a step back toward the earth, another, yes.

For the Soft God Paula

1. Trust Me

I have been here before, but not today. The geese quack,
water rustles, trees and grasses wave as something hot
and clever floats by, dizzy with balm and joy and a flood
of endorphins. And behind it all, shimmering, the soft god
I call Paula. Today she murmurs, she is happy: yes, she says,
your feints and bluffs are working, though only as long
as you worry about them. And if I do we can begin, can't we?
Or at least pretend that blond light really wafts across
this pond, that the geese in their dim-bulb way clack
and flutter in real time, that the sliver of quartz
on my wrist is counting in the right direction? I can't
tell names or dates but I believe these fragile insects
edging around me would taste awful if I swallowed them.

2. This Was In 1964

Why I do I still lean toward toys and games, why does it hurt
so to lose, why do I like feeling sore the next day? *If
I carried . . . If I carried the world . . .* the phrase starts,
but won't resolve. If I fit this place well enough, what
would I learn? This page? There's nothing here about
my running shoes, the caffeine in my system, the near-fight
my wife and I had in bed last night. There's nothing here
about Paula, who is real of course if only in my hazy head,
three parts yearning for the blazing silent wonders
of the world, one part the girl who sat across from me
in seventh grade. We whispered and passed notes that year
in an oddly childish way, considering she had the biggest
breasts in the class and was already getting cornered
by the town kids on hot summer afternoons. Yes she was real,
her smart-ass grin and cheeky swagger, not my best friend
but my friend, someone I could laugh with and not have
to touch, that last year before my hormones kicked in.

3. Or Any Name You Choose

She's elsewhere by now, not dead I don't think, I don't know.
And yes, I have no right to latch my clumsy yearnings onto
some made thing with her name, to make what I can't understand
into the feminine. But this is not about rights, it's about
the country that has me surrounded, its currents and murmurs
and wafty breezes, its brush and touch, its flesh and bones
and shivering surfaces. I should know by now, right? If
I carried the world would it comfort me, would it give me
an edge? Would it light me up soft as the last sun lights
the blushing bushes at the shore, the ragged cattail
like a torn cotton swab? It's lucky sometimes not to count
your change, not to play any game but the big one, to dream
only of Paula. Oh you blues, you crows, oh the slight black lace
that thins at the margins of sight, either tearing or healing.

"The Universe Is a Safe Place for Souls"

All right then. So what about Gary Eden, my archenemy all through junior high and the last person I ever fought in the serious physical sense? He was the best athlete in our class, but being a north-of-town Lutheran he got into hot cars and beer and never went out for anything after eighth grade. He wasn't all that vicious, but blond, lean and good-looking in his simple way, and bigger, stronger, faster and dumber than I was.

For years off and on I went around in fear of his picking at me, stealing my basketball when we were shooting around before practice, snapping wet towels at me in the locker room, driving me near and beyond tears long after I thought I was too old for that. Finally once in the locker room he stopped and looked at me oddly and almost seemed to change. He held his hand out. Sorry, he said. Sure you are, I said. No, I mean it, he said. Sure, I said, and looked at his hand. Sure you are. We got dressed. After that we quit fighting. We never talked. We were not friends. I don't know now if he meant it or not.

—for Jim Sargent

Where I Grew Up

> *"Where the land is flat in all directions, the only relief lies in gullies. Where the land is flat, ambush doesn't work. It's hard to die young."*
> —Janet Kauffman

But every section road is blacktopped now
some with stop signs some without
and with the corn high in the heat
you can see exactly nowhere at the corners.
I used to slow down in the summer
and coast through at thirtyfive or forty
only a little afraid of God and the police.

And so I understand about the three guys
from Gridley who started back a mile
to see how fast they could cross route 24
on a slow Friday early in football season
with the town in a television stupor
a twelve pack of empties in the ditch
a Nova that would do ninetyfive
only wandering a little and the corn
ripping past like half a tunnel.

Flat means something to us here.
There are ways to hide the hill folk
haven't dreamed of yet. The ambush worked
like John Wayne's gun and our boys found
their sweet relief and hard gospel
on the sweaty air and nobody
to argue how many rivers to cross.

Where I grew up the good farmers
have filled and seeded the gullies
into green obedient waterways.

Where I grew up we hate people telling us
how bad we've got it, how deprived.
When we leave we find other plains
or plant crooked rows of green beans
and kill every weed we see.

We teach our children all the stories
of the blizzards and tornadoes,
the droughts and the black deep soil,
its grand slow rolls only idiots
and easterners could call flat—
how we love it, how we hate it,
how it did not quite kill us young.

Walking Beans

1.
To do it right you must slow down, break your stride, refuse to just keep moving. The buttonweeds can fade right into soybeans; only the little points on the leaves and the color, barely more yellow, give them away. "When I find one," my father says, "if I turn and look back, seems there are always two or three more." I try it; he's right.

They aren't bad here, just a scattering, except in the tire tracks where the weed killer doesn't work as well. I say that I wonder why, and Dad laughs, "So do a lot of people." With the chemicals it's better than it used to be. When I was at home the bad patches were more weed than beans; we'd hack and hack for a hundred yards at a stretch, leave the spindly rows of beans poking from the pungent, green wreckage and say, wishfully, "They'll bush out." It was always hot, it seemed, and humid, and no shade even on the ends, and a half-mile round would take most of the morning. We begged and wheedled and tried to avoid it all through July and most of August, but they had to get done.

2.
My mother said to me once, "That was where it started, your poetry, don't you remember?" And I didn't, until she told me again about Kathy and the prickly little weeds we called bull nettles. "Blue metals?" Kathy asked once, forgetting for a minute to whine about the heat, her hoe dug into the earth to sit on. With bean leaves under my cap to keep my head cool I wrote my first song, for Kathy, the little sister I picked on far too much:

> I've got the blue metal blues,
> I'm as blue as I can be.
> I've got the blue metal blues,
> Everybody's picking on me.

3.
Near the road I spot something in the dirt and pick it up. A broken piece of plate, sea-green, fine ridges on the top rim and heavier waves on the underside. I remember then the house and buildings that stood on this forty, where my parents lived the first year of their marriage, just before I was born. I could be walking over the spot where they made love and made me.

The house I barely remember, small and shaded and empty, but the barn we tore down when I was fourteen, and it seemed we spent all summer putting boards across saw horses and banging the rusty nails through. The gray siding and two-by-tens would spring and jump like grasshoppers, and then we'd turn them over and strain out the bent brown iron with crowbars. We got hot, complained, threw nails at the bucket in the grass and missed, piled the boards slowly in the pickup, and finally got to quit and sit in the back of the truck as Dad slowly drove the two miles home. Some of that lumber is in our bookcases now, some still stacked in the barn at home, getting older, gray but still sound, waiting to find a use.

4.
I leave for home, grown up and on my own, bean-walking just a nostalgic interlude. Ten days later I am washing my feet in the tub after a softball game, when I suddenly remember washing them under the tap outside after walking beans, the same splash of cold water sluicing away the fine dust that sifts through sneakers and socks. And then I remember my father washing my feet at church on the night when my friends all somehow got paired up, and I was left over. I must have done his first, because when he finished he stood up and put his hands on my cheeks, hard, and kissed one of them, and whispered in my ear, "God bless you," the only time he ever said anything like that to me.

His Name Was Gerdon and He Ran a Hatchery in Graymont, Illinois

He was alone that day, the letter said,
and Sunday after church he stopped
by a cornfield, the sun warm and the wind
stirring up the crisp blank sounds
that rise when stiff leaves meet.
But those are my words. What my grandfather
wrote to my uncle was nothing so literary
and self-conscious. Once my uncle read
the letter to me, and said he'd send a copy.
He hasn't, though he wrote to say he'd tried,
but it was faint, in pencil, hard to copy.

It was my grandfather's last year, and
the death music ran under the words like
a muddy prairie creek. His heart was bad.
He knew. But he stood there, his hands
in the pockets of his baggy pants, and felt
the hand of God was moving in the wind.
You can really feel him there, he said,
on a hot Sunday in the country, with nothing
for miles but you and the corn and the hot earth.
He said it better than I have, though
I can't remember how. I lived
ten miles away, and saw him every week,
but never knew he had such thoughts.

He died in his sleep, in October.
I came home from college with my hair long,
and didn't cry, and went back. And now
I am settled in Ohio and his letter
is still with my uncle in Bakersfield,
too faint and faded to copy well. And so

I put this down, to claim what I can,
to hoard for some cold day to come
my uncle's hoarse voice reading
the shaky pencil on cheap blue-lined paper.
My uncle's name is Gerdon, too.
And out in the country between us
a road lies between fields, a ditch
on either side, and above it moves
something like a music, like a birth.

Seams

I. Waking in the Wrong Room

Where land and water meet the water ends,
the land goes under. I feel the tug toward
the depths, tell myself I'm too adult,
and go on yearning. What is real if not
the world inside my head? Remember snake-grass
in the swamps at camp, the way it pulled
apart in sections you could fit together,
the seams invisible and snug?

These planes drone on so capably I've only
seen one crash, and that while I was sleeping.
Only once I had the dream of waking
in the wrong room, and had to lie back down
and tell myself to sleep again, and wake up
right this time. It seemed to work.

II. On the Border

We wanted signs and slogans, wonders. What
we have are games. Form a line and find
your self and get it straight and keep it that way.
Every time I tell you to do something
don't until you say Mother may I.
Then do it.

                    The creek's been up and partway down;
now it's relaxed again, skimmed with ice
along the south bank. Take a deep breath
and look up to the glow of woods in fall,
nearly ready to abandon all that's left

to do. Little birds and squirrels use
the last light. Sit still, be slow, remember.

Any heat you thought to bring must be
forgotten. Any ice must melt. Any
grief or fretful wonder at the ways
God feeds his flock must not be bartered or
held back. You are an instrument ordained
to settle something. Your heart is strong,
your nerve fair. If your luck holds your children
may grow up safe on the couch, studying
catalogs, moaning for the seas of desire,
ordering anyway.
                     If you must worry
something, worry where your deeds are
registered. Worry why you just imagined
the figure a man makes as he shifts
into the gunsight.
                    See the red-tailed hawk
that just found dinner in the pond. See
the hill's curve, like a fine rump,
too big and dark for you to hold. Feel
the seam of earth and sky, how every moment
you are on the border. This won't last.
The giants will return, and pity us,
and say we can go with them if we find
our mothers, if we ask them first. And if
we find them, they will say we can.

Rhapsody with Dark Matter

(2000)

Rain

And a stray face spins me back to the black-haired girl
I saw long ago and stood helpless
watching her pass, bareheaded in the rain,
the easy way she found, wet but not hunched
against it, hair damp and shining on her brow,
her shoulders. I wanted to give something
for the dark rain of that hair,
the quiet of her face, not angry or restless,
alert to each step, the crowded sidewalk . . .
But what? Words? Dark rain. Wet face.

She never saw me. We've tramped on down
our own dark tunnels now for years. What hapless watcher
at my gates would know her face, would let her in
without the password, find her a bed, say rest,
sleep, I'll be outside?

I know. It shouldn't matter
who's lovely in the rain and who isn't.
But it's not beauty or nostalgia or even lust
that's got me, I don't know what it is,
justice maybe, prisons and churches, the glowing creatures
in the center of the sun. Most days I think
I'm almost free, I don't miss a single meeting,
I don't hit squirrels with my bike. Most days
it doesn't rain, and nobody walks the streets
in black hair, a light jacket and a glaze
of shining water, rain beading and touching her
all over like the hand of someone very large
and very gentle, very far away.

Hunger

"For this I have abandoned all my other lives."
                            -Robert Francis, "Waxwings"

Who could argue from this broad front porch in Camp Hill,
Pennsylvania, the mountain across the way, primrose blooming
just a day after snow, doves and sparrows in the trees

and Julia looking out to see if I'm hungry. I say no
just because it's so fine here with the cardinals chasing
and chirping for love or territory, the smart things

I might have said this afternoon, the sawdust from upstairs
where David is fixing bookshelves. They've been living here a week.
I can't stay past tomorrow but for now I'm not moving.

Last night we talked too late. This morning we packed books
from the basement, saving only the best ones, Jackie and Lee
in Europe, a colored sketch of brave Teddy Roosevelt

watching the lion maul a hapless native. Hunger and territory.
Guns and love. The air above the mountain is complete,
invisible, impure. My head feels hard and light

as those puffy mints that collapse on your tongue.
The writer insisted we can't say, "That table isn't there."
God either. Or the porch. Can we say where we stand

in the world, in anybody's heart, in the foamy eyes of God?
There's sun on the mountain, a city between it and me.
Yes, I'm hungry. I eat and eat and never does it last.

Breakfast at the County Seat Café

Someone turned the house into two dining rooms with the kitchen between, this smallish one crammed with the end of the morning rush, construction guys fueling their achy get-it-done bodies, older men in no special hurry, waitresses bustling among us all. The only space is at the counter right next to the register, last place I'd choose—I always want my back to a wall.

But the grandmotherly waittress talks to me, brings more bad coffee than I want, and I tune in to the hum and buzz and feel all right. The eggs are big and cooked just so and I eat the first piece of toast with them and the second with the blackberry jam.

The guys stroll up to pay their $3.94 or 68 cents for just coffee and maybe they notice me and maybe not but it's safe as churches, I know I can say no thanks next time the coffee comes around, I can pay and get out the door before my stomach muscles clench entirely with caffeine and the familiar strangeness of life a hundred miles from home at the County Seat Café.

When the rush slacks off the waitresses wash and dry, talk about another woman, the mall, some story. "She thinks I'm telling stories? She knows more about me than I know about her!" "That's right!" "I don't know anything about her!" That's right.

I love the hidden hollows inside rooms, inside language. I love to sit like a rock in the stream and wonder at the burbling around me. I love the exclamation mark, the dash, the waitresses bumping hips as they crowd past each other with plates of eggs and sausage. I love that half-laugh, the worlds inside it, the coins swept off the counter and the near-clean rag behind, yellow gloves and bruises at the hip and thigh, one more morning of men who need food and coffee and talk and are willing and able to pay.

The Sadness of Water and Women

1.
How many lies can the wrens
and cardinals try

before they find
the one to save them?

Who wouldn't want to be
the favored son?

Twists of last year's grass.
The heavy water sprawled and chill.

The red and yellow swirls
the leaves will soon crawl through.

2.
Go out easy. Pick the feet up.
Breathe and wait. Is it control you need?

Some praise? A good rest? Tell a story.
Once I told a story. Once

we hugged in the hospital room
and when I left the door locked behind me.

You still don't get it. Who
gets it. Tell your fear. No, show it.

Oh no. Let's have a joke,
an anecdote, let's say how the thin clouds

tip away from darkness, how
the new shoots rub themselves awake,

how the boys yell up behind me.
My friends are all stressed, tired

or crazy but I'm OK, it's Friday,
burgers on the grill.

3.
It's easier to love each other
when the world allows it. When three girls
are dancing on the stones. When for years
you've listened to the choir
and known the highest, sweetest voice
was coming home with you.
When she says *it's just so hard
out there* and you say, where?

4.
What to do when you need a word
when all you know is the sadness of water

and women and your own guilty joy
when the quarry changes color changes shape

everywhere your eyes glance off it
when the nurse comes to say it's time

and the door clicks shut

what to do

declare survive suppose
adjust hush

forty-four degrees
the sun still lying low

the red-splashed duck churns gently off
the heron blank and sober as a sword

hauls its lanky bones at last
toward some other shore

tomorrow the women will still be sad
tomorrow the water will still be blue

Old Water

If I had known, if I had known, would I ever
have thought to cross the bridge, to
shuck my clothes and slide into the quiet water?
In the fall, leaves languid on the cool lip
as the girls who'd never look at me.
Oh please . . .

When I went under what was waiting
touched me wrist and thigh and held firm,
strong, and settled deep with me.
I was desperate, then wild and then
my panic drifted off like an old whiff of skunk
and left the new stars dazzling, scent
of oniongrass and violets, the shape below me,
warm and smooth, the body nestled
inside the intimate water.
You could be so free, it whispered.
You could be so good.
I could not speak--and yet
I said, *Not this way*. I said
Not this time. What did I mean?
I could barely think of apples and children,
another life, and then the voice . . . *All right.*
All right. You won't go far.
                              Do I remember
after that? Mud, the hard sticks,
light splayed along the surface. Damp clothes
and my hands among them. Then traffic
and trees and this step, that step, thin
rusty slats of the stairs leading down.

So it's all about God, is it, or else not,
or else it's me and the stream I yearn toward

day and night, hour and year,
the stream I can hear and almost see
as two lovely women swing past
on the other trail.
They do not see me
and I let them go. But oh,
the beautiful saunter
of those women deep in their talk.
They walk the path up the mountain
and the old, old water tumbles down,
tumbles down.

—for Julia and Ginny

Rhapsody with Dark Matter

What's moving on the hills could be mist or rain
the first long notes of the apocalypse

or just another load of thick summer dreams.
What's coming won't be hurried or put off.

Yes the stars are out there, blazing, and all
the dark matter too. A woman with son and daughter

settles in beneath a bridge, smooths cardboard
with a dirty hand. A man pours beer and brags

of the tank he drove into the desert. Two million bucks.
So much easier to blow things up than get them right,

a marriage, a country, a small town forty miles
from the nearest beer. It isn't just this poem

that's loose, gliding from scenery to disaster,
floating through the gorgeous, deadly world.

It's not just me. Say what you will about the dark—
it won't leave you contented, or alone. It saunters

at its own pace down the long bluff, up the streets
of the finest little town in Arkansas. I'm trying

to remember where the keys are, which road I'll take
out of town. Remembering a voice: *I'm tired, yes.*

The boys are fine. Call Tuesday. Bring yourself home.

The Little Clerk

Sunday morning, ten o'clock, north through the greening,
partly ruined hills. Miles of thin grass behind the sign

for the Consolidated Coal Company, no fences, nothing moving.
Then cattle in a scrubby draw, black cow calmly grazing the ditch.

In the restaurant I asked dumb questions: Do you like Chicago?
Do you have sons? We both have sons. Do you feel grief,

you asked, when you think of them? Not *about* them, *of* them?
We talk and talk, we do, and then when it matters we go slow

and awkward, hoping not to disappoint. Still you seemed to me
a brother, lost for generations. What should we need to say?

It's all trying to become nobody, you said. I hate religion.
What is the ground of language, if not prayer? This must sound crazy.

You said, You still go to church when you don't have to?
And were impressed, envious maybe. I said I'd stopped trying

to escape, I said I've only almost surrendered. In Holmes County,
crows harry the red hawks. Tourist farms loll among the strip mines.

Three young men in gray stocking caps and plain clothes pump
their bicycles up the highway towards town. We're *not* separate,

you said, we're just *not*. Now you're on a plane, I'm here
with my windows rolled tight, music and coffee and the country

rolling by like a silent movie or the set for the rest of the story,
or the suit the jailors bring for the great man to wear before

the governor. Just before they bring him in the little clerk bends
to tie his shoe. The cup on the dash basks in the sun, so clear,

the slight green flecks, the whirls of brown, the glaze webbed
and crazed, clinging hard. I pick it up, I drink the coffee, still hot

and good. I swing onto the ramp and it slides an inch, adjusting,
as though it's learned some small, precious secret, and from now on . . .

—for Li-Young Lee

The Cookie Poem

"Here are my sad cookies."

The sad cookies. The once and future cookies.
The broken sweet cookies. The cookies
of heartbreaking beauty. The stony cookies
of Palestine. The gummy and delicious
olive and honey cookie. The pasty
damp cookie trapped in the child's hand.

Sad cookies, weird cookies, slippery
and dangerous cookies. Brilliant helpless
soiled and torn cookies, feverish and sweaty
cookies. Sullen cookies, sassy cookies,
the cookies of tantrum and the cookie of joy
and the sweet dark cookie of peace.

The faithful cookie of Rotterdam. The wild-eyed
cookie of Münster. The salty Atlantic cookie.
Cookies in black coats, in coveralls,
in business suits, cookies in bonnets
and coverings and heels, cookies scratching
their heads and their bellies, cookies utterly
and shamelessly naked before the beloved.

Cookies of the Amish division, cookies
of the Wahlerhof, cookies of Zurich and
Strassburg and Volhynia and Chortitza,
Nairobi Djakarta Winnipeg Goshen.
Cookies who hand their children off
to strangers, who admonish their sons
to remember the Lord's Prayer, cookies
who say all right, baptize my children
and then sneak back to the hidden church anyway.
Cookies who cave in utterly. Cookies

who die with their boots on. Cookies
with fists, and with contusions.
The black hearted cookie. The cookie with issues.
Hard cookies, hot cookies, compassionate
conservative cookies, cookies we loathe
and love, cookies lost, fallen, stolen,
crushed, abandoned, shunned. Weary
and heroic cookies, scathingly noted cookies,
flawed cookies who did their best.
Single cookies, queer cookies, cookies of color,
homeless cookie families sleeping in the car,
obsolete cookies broken down on the information
highway. Sad cookies, silent cookies,
loud cookies, loved cookies, your cookies
my cookies our cookies, all cookies
God's cookies, strange sweet hapless cookies
marked each one by the Imago Dei,
oh the Father the Son the Mother the Daughter
and the Holy Ghost all love cookies,
love all cookies, God's mouth is full
of cookies, God chews and swallows and flings
hands wide in joy, the crumbs fly
everywhere, oh God loves us all.

How the Boy Jesus Resisted Taking Out the Trash

O there's not enough to bother with.

O in a couple thousand years the landfills will be groaning.

O we're too poor there isn't any trash.

O what about Naomi what does she do around here.

O if ever you suspected what's to come you'd put me in the best chair, you'd kill the last kid for supper and feed me the heart and the liver.

O not now.

O remember my father's business and all that. Priests and Levites are going to love me, some. Locusts will sing and sizzle. Precious stones will roll toward me like mice. Everybody's pretty daughters will cry because I don't like them that way.

O I'll change it into figs and honey later, all right?

O all right.

Ancient Themes #1: The Martyrs & the Child

this is really pretty cool isnt it
leaving it all out but the letters wow
itll confuse my mom & piss off my teachers
so bad i always wanted to be bad or at least
i thought i was bad anyway i cant forget
those sunday school teachers
bernice for example my moms cousin
there we all were in the church basement
i was 10 years old maybe & shes asking
if we are ready to die like the martyrs
get our tongues screwed & fingers splintered
get burned up like firewood to heat
the hearts of those left behind well
thats some question when youre 10
in the middle of america in 1962
already scared of dying aglow
with radiation never mind with zeal
for the lord so there i sat gulping
& stalling with only those flimsy
beige curtains between our class
& the others with only a floor & a ceiling
& several miles of sky between me
& god leaning down to listen
& then my cousin connie who later went
wild & beautiful said she would do it
she would die for jesus yes she would
& bernice seemed pleased & forgot to ask
the rest of us & so i blundered on
into the rest of my life sweating out
the nuke tests & the bullies & the wondrous
heedless girls treading the tender grass
of my stupid young heart & i was surely
not so much worse for being forced

into uneasy contemplation of the fiery
heroes of old of the godless commies
& whether indeed i was ready to go up
in pain & splendor for jesus for believers
baptism for dirk willems turning back
half crazed with love for his pursuer
half full of pious shit surely clear
full of some weird lust to leave
this world & head out on the ice not
the canal not the lake no the true crazy
buckling thin ocean of ice jesus laid down
behind on his way out of town follow me
follow me well are you coming or not

                  —for di brandt

The Black Father

Not my real father still known as Whitey for his hair
for his open grin for his way of rubbing his head between
his work-thick hands when tired or embarrassed
but the father with secrets the black-haired father

the big smart father who learned to fly
who journeyed west & came home sad & triumphant
& filled with mysteries the black father agreed
to be the chosen one and he learned to speak in two voices

one used the old words few and strong the bible the vision
the stern & narrow way the other voice he kept
in his dark suit in an inside pocket held between chest
& arm too tight to slip out I guessed we guessed

at what wild secrets that voice knew we argued & proposed
but the suit stayed on the arm stayed down
the first voice kept talking it talked well
it had stories dramatic & perplexing

the last refugees pushed off the plane
the engines roaring to lift the groaning exiles
above the trees the father trembling at the stick
& we hushed & trembled & pondered what did that mean

while the father slipped away to answer one more
hard narrow letter about what some young fool
said on a weary Tuesday what some young body
did Saturday night on the gym floor

the black father didn't have it easy he gave
a lot up he learned to choose his moments
& his fights & kept whole reams of careful argument
in his secret drawer for centuries

well years anyway   in my last year the black father
had the class over & I stood near him & tried to say
that he had taught me something I was twenty
& from the country & I faltered & for a second

he seemed ready to speak but then just looked
down & turned away   it was not his fault
I was shy & young   bold only at the wrong moments
& maybe he was shy too but oh black father

I want to know what it was you almost said
what that inside pocket held & why you turned away

Letter to J. from the Ramada Inn
Western Avenue, Albany

Here's what I think: God wants us all
to love each other, but even God is not
sure how. We're still more in the dark,
so as you always say it's hard. We have
to learn how to be friends, true and mostly
apart, entangled with all our various others.
But today I'm bent toward sentiment and hoping
for indulgence as I offer thanks for having
taught me all that stuff I thought I knew
just wasn't so. I've tried to listen.
I've watched you flip your hair back
like a soft cape, hunch and get me
with those eyes and say OK, here's the thing.

And there are lots of things. In Albany
the hard spring project is underway.
I crossed the highway to the campus,
took the path around the pond, new leaves
hesitating out, crunch of my shoes
on the path, each step easier. I'd been
inside too long. A charming woman
with a terrier smiled and tugged
the leash. A crow vectored this way,
another that way. The signs pointed
to Colonial, State, Freedom.

The shuttle driver told me he'd lived
in Hamilton and Chicago but he liked
Albany, less muggy than the Midwest,
less snow than Watertown. His best friend
from high school talked him into moving here,
left in six months for San Diego. *I was*

in Chicago, he said, *a bad job and basically
no life, I got a driveaway, loaded half
my stuff, got another back and worked
a week for money and got another and loaded
up the rest.* He was casual and deft, making
the turns, telling his story, ponytail
and coffee. He waited for me at the airport
longer than he would have had to.
I gave him three bucks and said thank you
and wondered what I'd done to deserve my life.

I asked if all your other male friends
were gay and you laughed and said, mostly,
swinging down the street. As if.
You know how it is, saying things that
are more or less true and also way wrong?
It's my main talent, some days.

So how do we get from colonial to freedom?
Is there talk that's also action, words
to change the world? My father never talks
to women who aren't relatives or married
to him. Most of the people I can talk to
are women, most of them married to someone else.
From the fifth floor of the Ramada
the view is clear but mixed, yellowy
streamers of a big weeping willow,
shabby balconies of the Capitol
(from $39.00) Lodge. Everybody's gone
but me, I took this late flight back
saying it was cheap but secretly
wanting this six hours alone and free
to be silent and selfish, to choose
my own steps.

                    One window's almost
clear, the other etched and streaky.
Three flags—US, Canada, Ramada—
keep trying to find some accommodation
with the wind. I could drink the whisky
I didn't drink with the boys last night
but I'd rather have coffee. This is taking
longer than I thought. I always want
to think things aren't so bad, you always
want to fix them.
                    You taught me that
I trust myself too much, you made me listen,
talk wise and dense as cherry or mahogany.
You can't drive nails through such wood
and finally I laid my hammer down, though
it's still in the toolbox.
                         When I put
new strings on the old Martin,
twist and fiddle and scratch a few chords
and fiddle until they settle in, there's
a moment when I know it's ready.
I pick the low E, the A and the sound
opens, something wide and new and full,
some space I can never enter before
it flickers out, not gone, just
thinned past what my clumsy ears
can gather. I touch the notes and yes,
they rise again. And then I stop--
it seems so odd and big a gift, this
beat-up scratched-up D-18 that's mine to play
because Marlyce's grandparents got it
from a crazy cousin worried that the *bengels*
would steal it. I don't deserve it but I savor it,
I play D, G, E minor, C, A minor, I tinker up
the neck, I know a hundred songs by heart but
I have to stop and wait for what to play.

So here I am, stalling, tinkering, waiting
for some body to start muttering in my left ear.
This is all about me. You have no truck
with this mushy mystic stuff, when I show you
the poems I don't get but can't abandon
you don't get them either. It's all just
spiderweb and guesswork and semi-truths anyway.
All of your male friends are gay. All
of my women friends are secretive luminous
and troubled, they talk all the time
and teach me incredible things but only
very slowly, I forget the simplest ones over
and over. Even this is wrong. Especially
this. At best a few of my opinions
have blown over in the big storms like poplars
or chinese elms, fast-growing but flimsy.
The hard oaks and maples are still scrubby
and weak, inching their way toward heaven.

Some make it, some don't, and what
does that mean? Long ago Nick told me
*You? You don't want to compete,
just win.* And even before that, first grade,
Mrs. Johnson: "Jeff likes to be a leader
but needs to learn to let others be leaders."
And Jeffers: "What but the wolf's tooth whittled
so fine / The fleet limbs of the antelope?"
Fear and desire. What else? "Sports may not be
a very good way to learn anything about life,"
you told me, "it's not very helpful when
you try to compare anything." Maybe not.
I don't understand the ethics or aesthetics
of soccer or poetry or life. But when
I try to call timeout, nothing stops.

There are lots of things, few of them pure,
many of them good. It's no easier
for me to quit figuring where I stand
than for you to quit wondering how
your hair looks. How hard to move rightly,
to avoid the old tracks. Three times
I found myself on the same path around
the pond, scenic but not getting me
any closer to home. How many times
have I made that old round through desire
and propriety. How hard to say things straight.
*Nothing that is said clearly can be said truly
about the gods* wrote that old pantheist
C. S. Lewis. How easy to love and how hard
to love well, how little we know and how
much we get wrong and still carry the other
in heart and mind and belly, sit
in the weird bar with white tablecloths
and dozens of TV screens through
the strange afternoon, whisper and laugh
and contend and then walk up the hill
to the big bad hotel and the crowd of friends
and strangers just inside the door.

There's space for many loves in any heart
if we learn to let them in and out,
to roll and carry them like shirts,
like books we buy and haul back home,
heavy but precious, dense and dangerous
as radium, the pages whispering in
the whistly dark of the baggage hold,
six miles above the ground, swift and
precarious as anything that must be owned
and shared at the same time. God wants
us all to love each other. But only
very slowly can we teach each other how.

What the Prairie Boy Learned on the Whistler Road

In mountains there's only one way home. Drive
or let somebody else. In mountains all deliberations
end in aesthetics or triage.

In mountains you don't need faith to believe that God
is both sublime and funky. Phrases like inscrutable workmanship
make sense. Of *course*, you say, souls can be washed clean.

At this coast the islands are mountains with wet feet,
their heads dizzy in the late haze. They get up early
but laze through the day, sure there's another coming.

In mountains a blue-black rock loomed in its fogs,
dire and high-toned as a desert prophet. One glimpse,
all I could spare, then back to the cars, the signs, the next curve.

It was enough. Where I live there are no mountains. Lack
is the father of beauty. Beauty is the father of the mountains.
The mountains are the father of everything.

Greatest Hits

(2003)

The Archetypal Experience
of C. Wordsworth Crockett

He went out
pome hunting,
wandering his decidedly
altered perceptions through
an area of trees
grass flowers birds
and other natural and/or
organic items among which
pome hunters of a certain stripe
have down through history found
their finest and most annotated pomes.

He craftily ignored
the first few trivial soft
malnourished pomes to be seen
creeping timidly about, in an instant
knowing them for runts and rejects
the taking of which
was not so much forbidden as despised

but having wandered for a time
sufficient to have kindled
in his breast those emotions
of rage despair and yes,
most terrifying, boredom,
to which pomehunters are
most vulnerable,
our hero spied a somewhat modest
but well structured pome beginning
"Leaves had browned / among the
branches where" and culminating in
a carefully unstudied metaphor

relating the uncertainties and
gradual growth of a most
uniquely mediocre tree
to questions of ontology
epistemology and yes life itself
in words of no more
than two syllables,
shot it down
and dragged it home.

How to Write the New Mennonite Poem

Choose two from old Bibles, humbly beautiful quilts,
Fraktur, and the *Martyr's Mirror* in Dutch.
Get the word "Mennonite" in at least
twice, once in the title, along with zwiebach,
vareniki, borscht, and the farm,
which if possible should be lost now.

Grandmothers are very good, especially
dead grandmothers, especially speaking
German in Russia. They should have
Suffered. Mothers are good and may
have Quirks, if lovable. Male ancestors
are possible but presumed to represent
the patriarchy and to have abused
"their" wives, children, farm animals;
steer clear unless you are Angry,
or can supply affidavits from
everybody who knew them.

It is important to acknowledge
the spiritual and reproductive
superiority of plain coats and
coverings, the marvelous integrity
of those uncorrupted by television
and Mennonite higher education.
Use quaintness, brisk common sense
and a dash of barnyard humor to show
that they are Just Folks Too.

Remember that while the only good Mennonite
is not a dead Mennonite, many dead
Mennonites were really good. Work in
two or three. Dirk Willems
is hot this year. Include a woman,

an African if you know any, and
a Methodist with redeeming qualities.

You, of course, are a backslidden,
overlearned, doubtridden, egodriven
quasibeliever who would be less anxious
and surer of salvation if you could
only manage to give up the car,
the CD player, and coaching soccer.
You really *want* to be like Grandma.
You believe in discipleship, granola,
and the Peace Tax Fund, but things are
Complicated. You think about them plenty.
You plan to give up something, soon.

If you're in a major city, which
you should be, say something about
the streets, how you really hate
the place but get all charged up
walking around on your days off
looking at stuff and drinking
exotic coffee. Mention that this
seems strange to you, as does
the fact that sometimes you like sex,
even when you know the people in
the next apartment are listening.
Put your wedding ring in the poem
to reassure your parents.

Use the laser printer, and send
a large, glossy, black and white
photograph, just in case. Wear
something simple and dark. Smile
but not too hard. Let your eyes
reflect the miles you have come,
the centuries, your gratitude, your guilt.

Deerflies

(2004)

Deerfly

When I was a redwinged blackbird I knew every post and stump, I could tell exactly when it was time to fly.

When I was a water lily I gave all my best leaves to the pond, and my best blossoms too.

When I was a cattail I knew my friends and my numerous enemies by their scent and their shape and the size of their stems.

When I was the multiflora rose I found many cozy spots, I was thorny but hip, I was nicer to the bluebirds than the crows.

When I was the duckweed I stuck to any bird I could, half the time I didn't even bother with the flowers, just split whenever I got the chance.

When I was the pond I rested for weeks on end, let the wind and the sun do all the work, said *whatever* all the time.

When I was the sun I had many urgent and utopian ideas, I changed millions of tons of this into that, I didn't care who watched or burned themselves blind trying.

When I was the path everybody thought they used me, but they all went exactly where I led them.

When I was Jeff I walked some paths, sat beside ponds, listened to songs I couldn't name. During the eclipse I looked straight at the sun for an instant and afterwards I could still see, though never as clear nor as far as I dreamed.

When I was a deerfly I zoomed around every body's head, as if I could persuade them my troubles were their own.

Mumble

And my high-dollar ultralight runners are so thin at the ball
that any stray rock means a bruise. Let's not calculate
this economy of cash and waste, not while my feet still feel

the cobbles of Colmar and Rothenburg. Let's not complain
of the weekends spent sulkily at quiz bowl meets, the lost arches
where gleams the untraveled world. Say it's all one,

the dizzy traveler and the guy on the side yelling yes, yes
as his son puts the ball in the net and the one in thin lamplight
knurling back and forth on some stubborn sentence

as though enough wear would turn it soft as old denim,
dark and heavy as the Black Gate of Trier where Simeon
had himself walled right in for seven years, as if to prove

that only the faithless fear simplicity. Oh let's believe
that all sounds rhyme, water spill and boys fishing and one bird
chirring like a knife on a plate. Let's pretend we can see

straight to the bottom of the lake. Let's pretend we can
say what we need and then someone will give it to us,
our one lost desire, the fat coils of steel that get

hurried down the highway, the shiny-eyed girl sauntering
up the path, the solid hand of Jesus yanking us out of the creek.
Let's reckon the history and geometry of driftwood

battered into radiance. Let's imagine we know the true word
for this life, for one duck and a silvery battered boat,
three men on the quarry and the mumble of afternoon traffic,

persistent and stunned as the leftover mutter of the big bang.

Black Cat in Byhalia

What can I say about all this, trees reaching up one at a time,
thousands and hundreds of trunks branches twigs stems
every bit in exactly its own single space, singular

and individual as the exit that I just missed in this hyperbolic
existentialist poetic trance. "Days go by in broken English"
you mutter on the tape, and oh they do. Out here they go by

without any kind of English, they just go, those trees
hold their hands up, the snow lays its easy fingers down,
everything else just flits and wobbles toward its own place,

everything has been changed by someone who isn't here now,
some set of guys who walked and tilled, plowed and planted
and strung together the power lines, phone lines, water lines,

guys who did their work and went home and left it, empty
and relentless as a cloud or the ocean a mile down.
They'll be back. Sekou, there's a lot of space here

but less room than you'd think. And there goes a huge flock,
2, 3, 400 birds moving like a stirred-up kettle,
a whirlwind of dark, small, crazy birds, splitting into parts

then whirling back together, the whole boiling mess
above one big bird, a hawk I think, all those little birds
like a black, beaked message from the God of the sharp little birds,

a sign for the hawks that out here even they had best watch
where they fly. And this is Byhalia, where the black sweet muck
grows the best white sweet Byhalia onions in the world,

where the houses seem to grow right out of the ground,
where the Evangelical Friends Church stands white and friendly
at the north end of town. And this is Mt. Victory

where I sail through a very yellow light at 33, 34 miles an hour
and nobody's coming fortunately and no police cars lurking
to drag me down and interrogate my clean white ass and so

I sail on into the countryside, past the hopelessly scenic
and defunct barns slowly crashing in like broken-down boats,
leaking those old prairie hopes of order and prosperity

and barns handed down to the children, barns that would hold
the warm dumb cows and tender sheep and hay heavy and sweet
in the loft above, barns that held the thickheaded dreams

of old men who wore themselves down getting up in the dark
to feed the stock before going to the fields, coming home
at dusk to feed the stock again, dog-tired, bone-tired,

tired to their souls and guts, and the wives waiting
with the beef roast still warm in the oven but dry, dry
and tough, and eating in the kitchen silence with the hard

overhead light bouncing on the formica table, the linoleum,
the white cupboards, nothing to say, knowing where
it was all heading, the boys gone off to the city

and the girls married to men who were drunk already every night,
men who knew only the wrong ways to use their hands.
And the barns run aground on the reefs of money and time,

the slowest and most cornily scenic shipwrecks in history,
old men dead in their dusty beds and the women dumped off
at the county homes where every morning the nurse

brings in the drugs, combs the white thin hair down over
the leathery foreheads and leaves the rest to tangle as it will.
I almost forgot, Sekou, but as I drove through Byhalia

with you asleep beside me there was this black cat, I saw it
coming on and I thought Come on, cat, you see me, you know
I'm big and heavy and you're not but this cat just kept on coming

and I could go nowhere and do nothing but run right over this cat,
right front wheel right rear wheel just like that, boomp, boomp,
and I looked back thinking Oh, no, thinking to see flat cat

all over the road. But here's this cat in the other lane,
tail a little ragged but all its legs working it across the road,
another car just misses, this cat is annoyed and ruffled

but not even limping, I swear this cat is thinking, "Man,
how many times do I have to get run over today?" It's looking
testy and bedraggled but the cat is walking, where this cat

is heading I don't know but that is one tough black cat.

—for Sekou Sundiata

Meditation in Glen Helen

*"Who knows what you know that you don't
know you know . . . you know?"*

So I went to the Yellow Spring, cupped the cold water
flowing from the red rock and tasted a little,
chill and metal-hard. So the park closes at dusk, and
I've been so much with people that for a while

I disremember how to be alone. So the summer trees unfold
around me, careful, steady, and two guys and a girl
peel their jeans and frolic in the pool below.
Oh, the water will splash. I have my questions.

I will stand together with the others lost and lame
when the time comes, cool at the edge of the river,
mudding my toes in the brown coarse sand,
crying with all the children: what is it I know,

how can the iron-clean water have so little to say?
The forest makes it easy to hide anything, an eyelash,
a brown long-limbed spider, the bones of the first man
to put a hand into the spring and say cold, say good.

Even the last ridge can hold the trees only so high.
Some of the paths are closed for reconstruction.
Some of the paths are broad and clear. Some days
I walk around and around my little town, fussing

at the tv haze, stumbling over the brick sidewalks
quietly being swallowed by the grass. Some days
I believe that everything can be stomped or outrun.
Some days only the highest bridges stand a chance

of surviving the floods. Some walnut trees
are lonely mothers, last year's crop all swept off
by the squirrels who broke the bony sheaths open
and chewed themselves fat on the oily, convoluted hearts.

—for Julia Levine

White Dog

Earth ending, I went free,
left all my cares behind
among the lilies falling and out of mind.
        -San Juan de la Cruz, "The Dark Night"

The mysteries of God, he learned, were spoken best
in images of tousled hair, cool fingers, dark meetings.
The knowledge of the evening, he called it.

Shut in the Priory at Toledo, half-starved, beaten,
he heard a love song rise from the street,
fragrant with the lover's ardent body.

He wrote "The Dark Night," and after eight months
he escaped down a hand-twisted rope.

*

Here I walk out in the daylight. I guess
my beloved is tangled in the branches nearby.
She has slept in her cool nest all winter.

I think tomorrow if the sun shines
she will wake and look about,
she will know it is time to find me.

*

A little more green appears each day,
the fields warm and the moon goes
a little fuller. The blackbellied jet slashes over,

low and loud. The young white dog
with the heavy shoulders ignores his lady's instructions.
If I were a dog, how far would I run?

Would I come when she called? Would I push
through the thicket of head-high saplings,
dirty my feet in the mud at their roots?

*

I am the one who has slept all winter.
I think I must walk out into the wet prairie,
scoop water from the spring,

climb the black maple as high as I dare.

Morning Song from Oneonta

Five hundred and eighty-two miles
east from home the dark comes early
but the dawn seems truly new

at the window of the east-facing room.
The goose protests with all he has
and two crows tell the neighbors

what matters and what doesn't.
Around my little fan the black,
frail insects lie like crumbs.

The yellow slash of a goldfinch now
in the high pine, no wind at all,
haze softens the hills and a pair

of swifts fly close, then part.
Ignorance is bliss, she said,
a hint of laughter in her voice.

I want the goldfinch to come back,
the haze to clear. In the perfect world
I would be asleep and dreaming

of the hills, of the unseen river
that winds among them. But in this huge
and hazy morning the poplar

and the pine sway and beckon
and I am awake and tired
and filled with sudden, crazy joy--

as if a quiet voice had said,
*See that orange roof, the house
with the little spire?*

If you want it, it's yours.

Instructions for the Night Walk

Cup your hands behind your ears and you'll hear
the water moving way below. Think deer, think bats.

Nothing paler and more poised than the young poison ivy.
Nothing deeper than the circle of the last pool left in the ravine.

Daisies in the half light, the clink of stones, sighs.
Somebody who speaks as the heron launches. Suppose

your father was a stony river, or some words
chanted in the half light while other letters traced

themselves in your head, insistent, out of nowhere.
Whatever comes next you won't expect it, won't deny it,

plain and eccentric as the buckled floor of the world,
your soul-bird settling to float easily downstream.

Suppose anything you need, and pay as much attention
as you have. Don't say anything. There are voices

that speak only once. Every leaf is singular. Touch
your right temple, where something might have landed.

Find nothing. Feel nothing and suppose you might rise
earlier than anyone ever has, selfish and complete,

listen to the brilliance of the gibbous moon, throw most
of yourself away and let what's left condense, go heavy,

spiral inward until it bursts into flame and wings away.
Don't wait. Don't falter. Don't say anything to anybody, yet.

Winds you cannot feel or imagine pass through every second,
tides of secret intelligence surge and ebb. There is honey

and red wine, hard bread and cheese on a plate. There are
empty boxes, cans without labels, the final storms.

If anyone asks say how empty you feel, and how full.
When they say choose a stone, choose a stone. When they say

put it down, don't say anything. But keep it in your hand.

—for Terry Hermsen

Ancient Themes: The First Teacher

An apple a day, keep the teacher away, that's what I learned
in those floor-tile days when lessons were hard pine
and shrill, sit down be still. You were tough and gnarly,

Mrs. J., you knew what you wanted and I wasn't even close.
I was snippy, mean, too smart by half, you were right
not to trust me. When the girls tittered and you snapped,

I told Mom things were fine. That cafeteria day when
you stretched your face at me I knew I'd need luck and nerve
to survive. At home I flopped with the Cat and Captain Jinks,

searching for the secret. If I cleaned it all up before
the grownups got home. . . But no. Years of intricate maneuvers,
hundreds of lapses and blunders, finally I wasn't so tiny.

Yes this is personal, hard as the pine tables of that long-gone
basement room where you broke every chunk of my soul
you could reach. I kept most of the pieces. They went back together.

It's time you get out of my head. All those years you lay cramped
in the smelly rest home I passed by and saw your name and never once
stopped. Even in that town where God's middle name is Listen

the buzz-cut boys are safe now. When I wake in a panic
I remember: *You didn't get me. You'll never touch my children.*

Second Morning Song from Oneonta

So early the black flies are still asleep.
A high scruff of rock where lovers

carved their names and then slipped back
into the soft needles under the trees.

Already the valley hums and crackles
and the last rolls of mist hang over

the smokestacks like those fine scratches
that pile up on your glasses. God said,

the places that please you will often
be difficult to find. God said, sweat

is a good sign but not reliable.
God said, hold this day like an egg,

hold and cherish it as you dream
of being touched yourself. Break the day

but gently as the great chef breaks eggs
for the dish you cannot name or afford.

God says all this has been given you,
the whine of the crane and the whir of engines

pulling tired women to their bad jobs
and the drumlin where the last glacier

gave up its journey and grumbled away.
God says remember, God says

don't give up. God says give up.

Brain Remembers Things That Did Not Happen
-Reuters Headline, 11/22/00

In the sixth year of the war I left my daughter
where I knew the enemy would find her.

I dug the last potatoes in the cold mist,
warmed by the work. Too often the spade
sliced the best ones, dirtying the white flesh.

In the fourth year of the war I traded my tools
for six cans of soup. Steak with potatoes, chicken corn chowder.

There was a high room behind and stage left,
we gathered late at night, carefully.

We should try to talk to them, she insisted.

In the third year of the war I made colonel. Me.

Could you slide that cup this way, she wheedled--
I hate the taste but I love the smell.

In the first year of the war we watched for hints,
sure that the end was near. The news, the birds.

Her first smile, like daybreak, just for me.

Anything you want. Anything.

The great white bear gliding, arms open like a mother.

Epiphany with Sirens and White-Tail

Almost dark and I should be going
but it's a green Christmas, or brownish

at least, even when sirens kick up suddenly.
Will we ever be safe? Not in this world.

In church today I watched the flame
of the candle suck and flicker, blew my breath

at the chimney and felt the old thoughts
of fire and time and death flare up.

Kill the boy-children of Bethlehem,
Herod demanded, and was obeyed

but found himself no safer or more content.
Another siren. Nothing stirs.

Branches still as children playing freeze tag.
Our goal is to secure the peace,

said the one who leads us, *voluntarily,*
or by force. He will be obeyed.

The sirens are finished for now
and the birds take back the air.

The white-tail floats through brush
like a half moon set free,

like a light on the path to Egypt
where the boy child will live out his exile

and return when the mad king is dead.

Letter from Ragdale to J.

I've seen three lost gloves on the trails--one purple, one blue,
and a leather work glove stuck lifelike and grasping on a branch

in the north lane. I almost took it just because it frightened me.
I come and go simple as rain, eat and drink what I please.

I sit at the table between the four windows and the door
to the porch. *I'm not all here*, she said, or was it *I'm not myself?*

The train rattles off through the rain. So many books--I gnaw
like a raccoon in the sweet corn, throw them down. Last night

it was *Let Us Now Praise Famous Men*, the need to bear
"the true proportions of the savageness of the world."

It's not hard to bear anything in this fine substantial place,
where people I don't know have paid my board and room.

Behind the house is the meadow, then the prairie, then the river
and the woods, the train tracks, the highway. The world

is very old. There are many hours in a life, many nights.
 I don't want to fall asleep. Past the train tracks there is

only silence and the cold of space. Past the cold space
there is nothing, nothing. On the other side of nothing

are a million creatures. They breathe and hunt, ripen
and fall. There is a crust on nothing and we call it sweet.

There is another and we call it low. There is another and we have
no word but we eat it, slowly, we must drink and breathe and

never see or know it, the walls of the house and the hard floor
and the sweat burning in the lovers' eyes and the wet muck

into which the seed is pushed, again, again, what use, go away,
God bless you, step in, go away, oh please, sit down, sit down.

Scenario

The aliens arrive, saucers white and gleaming like sails.
Their instruments are excellent and they all speak several
of our tongues. Still they confess to struggles with translation.

They bring peace, but not the peace we have imagined.
They have a story we must learn, a story that drives them
through the galaxy. There was a child, a king, prophets,

plagues, a horrifying death and a word more precious than
the world. They do not tell this story start to end, the word
resists all of our tongues, *red wolf racing in the dim forest?*

someone asks, no, *a vole in the meadow grass, meeting his beloved?*
No. They beg for patience, they are sure we can learn,
we may know as they know. In the meantime, they bring

other gifts. Centuries pass. They talk and we listen, when
we can. Millions die in the plagues they insist were accidental
and tragic. The gleaming towers they build for us stand empty,

the wide spirals they insist must crown each one screw themselves
enigmatically into the sky. They cannot go back, their ships
burnt dead by the deeps. More were to follow but none arrive.

They grow melancholic, distracted, they live for centuries
but do not breed--something in the sun, they believe.
We have the word, they die insisting, the only word,

the child told us there was no other word. They speak
the word, dying, reluctant, desperate. We listen. Nothing
changes. We bury them according to their ways, face up,

lightly covered, not too deep. When the child returns
in glory she will save us, they told us many times,
if we are covered lightly and not buried too deep.

Ancient Themes: The Spring at Ragdale

Two girls at the half-moon bridge, shy when I greet them
though one answers, hello. I walk on, but later
they are kneeling at the spring--to drink? to find their faces?

As I pass they stop me, they've just cleaned the spring,
a dog's been in it, they are happy now. Dana's father
built the stone rim a long time ago. Her blond hair flashes.

She's thin, maybe eleven, her friend Eileen is pretty too.
What are you, they ask, and I say I'm a poet and Eileen says,
Dana wants to be one, and looking down a little Dana smiles,

yes, she writes poems. Eileen wonders if I wrote a book
and so I say I'll give them one. We walk back, meet Dana's father
puttering outside, go on to the guest house. They wait

and whisper as I go upstairs. When I'm back Dana pulls out two bills,
crumpled--you've been so nice to us, she says. No, no, I tell her,
you've been nice to me. They lean to the book and pull it open,

thanking me as if I needed thanks when they're the ones
who cleaned the spring, when they told me what to do:
put your hand in, feel the bubbles, they go down and down.

You can drink it, Dana said, it's better than regular water,
and she cupped her hand and drank to show me how.

Ancient Themes: The Night

in the dark, where all goes right . . .
        -San Juan de la Cruz

A morning sweet with bird song and the low grasses
gathering themselves. Two crows on the lawn, the lane
a bit firmer with each dry day. Bench in the sun

at the edge of the winter burn, and a robin clucks
high in the oak grove. I wanted to say that the morning
is sad, that every time is sad, every thing, God

and the sturdy oaks and the oracular missiles
in their cool hidden tubes. Then I wanted to say
that only *now* is sad, its ashy surfaces and lone sheaf

of shivery bluestem. All the rest, before and after,
is something other, muddy and sharp at once,
a shelf of brilliant unread books, the undulant flight

of a cardinal toward its mate. And still the robin
only clucked, and the bluestem shivered, and so I say
what the poet said: The day is joyful, and so is

the dark night. If your love burns bright with yearning,
if you dress in the secret clothes and climb down
the hidden ladder, if you follow the fire in your soul,

then the lover will be waiting in the swaying cedars.

Small Night Song from Oneonta

It's good that the world has more beauty
than it needs. It's good to walk into
the smooth Catskill night and discover

that the night has no edges, no sympathy,
no grievance against me, that any place I step
will hold me firm, not like a lover,

not like a child. It's good to be a child,
and then for years to be something else,
and then something else. It's a hard world

but the rain is persistent, the deer
are quiet and discreet, and for ages now
the trees have known how to dream their way up.

A man with a pack on his shoulder
saunters down the path below me, knowing
the lights he sees ahead are burning for him.

Spoken among the Trees

(2007)

Damselfly

*Beginnings have an irritating but essential fragility,
and one that should be taken to heart.*
—Teilhard de Chardin

Consider that ant swarm on the sidewalk, like spilled brown sugar, and the pale yellow leaves the hackberry casts free in a dry June, pressed to the parking lot.

The gray uneven two-by-fours of the picnic table, no place to set a cup half full or half empty.

A green grain head, waving from the corner the mower can't reach.

Elijah's cloak parting the waters, and Elisha: "Let me inherit a double-share of your spirit." And Elijah: "Your request is a difficult one."

And the bowl with the coiled serpent in its heart. And *This is my body*. And the stones of the creek, surfacing with the drought.

When spoken, the secret is no longer the secret. I am not good at secrets. The God I love speaks only in roars and whispers. The God I love only seems to play favorites.

At nine it is already humid, and the woods are dressed in their seven summer greens. All around me the machines are sorting and sifting, cutting and burning.

I wait a whole minute and a black damselfly crosses the creek and the world begins again and again.

And far away right here in town, the child wakes and rolls and stretches, not yet hungry. Wide-eyed, he waves and coos to bring the day into his blue-tinted room.

And there she is, smiling in the open door.

Fulks Run to Cumberland

We were almost to Lost City when my companion said,
This is beautiful, but I'm so sleepy. Sleep, I said, knowing
I had the wheel and coffee in the mug, and soon

she was traveling blind beside me. I steered on
and refused every side road no matter how winding
and inviting, I let Maggies Creek Road and Narrow Lane

and Toms Knob Approach slide on by, I grumbled
only a little at the long stoplight at the one-lane bridge.
My companion was leaned way back, dreaming

of angelhaired lovers for all I knew, breathing
so easy I thought she must be hearing the sweet shoals
of the Lost River running low along the road, whispering

for half a mile before turning away as the hills said they must.
I obeyed every last curl in the road and turned up the stereo,
hoping my companion would awaken and speak: *I've been*

dreaming, you were there, goldenhaired angels were there,
we must go back and turn at Lost City, take the Narrow Lane
into the mountains. I saw a perfect seed head shaking

in the golden evening, every puff a signal and a sign.
Don't you remember what the river said as it caressed
the gray stones? Listen . . . but my companion only turned

and rode her slumber onward, leaving all the rest
to me. *Last night I dreamed that I was dreaming*,
sang the singer. A fluted hill, a long curve. On the lake,

five geese stirred, shook out their wings, and disappeared.

Advice for Walkers

Watch your step. You could fall any minute through
the hard skin of rock, the soft skin of dirt. You could find

yourself floating to an awkward reunion with the debris
you've been trailing behind you all these years.

Watch carefully. There are some who burn so bright
even a glance will leave you whirling. Watch the ground

at your feet and the last stretchy sky. There is much
in the mucky spring that you don't want to bring home

on your shoes. No one knows where the miracle
will begin, or where the disaster will start. No one knows

the name of the beloved until it is spoken, perhaps gently
when asked how to say it, Maria, or Kaitlin, or Grace.

The earth is a mirror. The sky is a lens. The trees are an echo
of their own roots, of your own roots, your lost fathers

brooding on shades of black in the quiet caves, your mothers
counting the one breath they manage each month, praying

thank you, praying goodbye. Watch your step, not the women
who glow like stars and are just as much your business.

Consider the small brick porch where your son lost his balance
years ago, where he fell hard, dizzy with love and hunger.

When your eyes have drunk a million shots of splendor
and turned back for more, when your heart has packed

and hidden every wonder, every slender ankle, every head
of curling invitations to the wrong feast, when desire

elbows memory into the bushes and runs headlong downhill
smack into the creek, when the creek closes icy

and astonishing over you, all your clothes soaked and useless,
the last veils of your secrecy torn open like the car door

after the crash, when you clamber up dripping mud
and snowmelt and the most obstinate futility since

second grade, when you fumble at the bank, scrape knuckles
on the frozen roots, on the slabs of broken ice, oh my friend,

lift your dripping useful boot and press it to the ground,
press and push and even now the world will hold you up.

The Recovery of Imaginary Friends

The guidebook of holy places lacks directions because
the places are holy, and when disturbed they move

somewhere else anyway. Still, consider the disturbing bison
on the cave wall, the reassuring handprint on the ceiling.

"We'll never know why the masks face inward," said
the tour guide, "but the people who made them know."

When the writer described her daughter's invisible friend,
I remembered my mother going on about Giffy,

my own lost companion, who did everything I shouldn't have.
All I know of him is what my mother tells the whole table

every other Christmas or so. Is it best to mourn
our imaginary friends or be glad to be shut of them?

I believe in holy places, both fixed and mobile,
and I believe in the lazy line of the Navajo rug.

I believe in Giffy, though he hasn't spoken to me since 1955.
I want the charismatic macrofauna to thrive

and the coral and honeybees, too. I want to bless
the unmedicated and the millionaire developers and to clean

the lead, mercury, and flame retardants from everybody's blood.
I want to know what Giffy's been up to, if he's happy,

stoned, depressed, working the night shift, solitary, gay,
pious, making cold calls or walking free and sweet through

some high canyon like the loose thread in a Navajo rug.

Late Psalm

> *Then David ran and stood over the Philistine,*
> *and took his sword and drew it out of his sheath,*
> *and killed him, and cut off his head with it.*
> —1 Samuel 17:51

It was dark when I left town and still dark when day had come, the sky and trees dulled and damp.

I remembered the preacher: Consider David and Goliath, he said, the two of them boasting of their strength and the God who loved them, both of them warning that the other's sweet body must fall bloody in the dust and be torn by dogs.

The children came up to hear the story told for them.

I drove through scant snow and the long spectacle of tree after tree after tree, each brown and gray in its winter simplicity, singular, alone and not alone. Then the Big Oak Church, like another easy growth.

Couldn't we name all the churches after trees and creeks?

I wanted some sunshine, but that didn't mean I would get it. I wanted some words as clear and sharp as swords, instead of a sword.

Flurries and sunshine breaking through, and suddenly the word *sublime* was in my head. I let a truck in ahead of me, passed another, headed down the long, curving hill.

And Jackson Browne sang, "He rescued truth from beauty and meaning from belief."

And the snowflakes seemed sparse enough to count, though I soon gave up.

There are many worlds, and they are all this world, held apart by thin braces of time and weather.

Sometimes you can spray all you want and let the wipers run, but the windshield just won't come clean.

Besides forgiveness there must be something else, something like abandon--going on without forgetting, without fear.

Abandoned, like the site of an ambush. Or the last camp on the way to the ambush. Or the place where a few hungry people stayed afterward, no water, no fire, just a place to lie down in the snow.

Interior Colloquy in Glen Helen

How long do I have? Forty-two minutes. Is that a path or a watercourse?
Never mind. These rocks are really slick. Can I crawl through

the waterfall and into that little cave? Somebody must have.
What would James Wright say? Will I ever settle down?

What you mean "I," white man? Lunch will be good. Walk
a little more. Rhododendron, heavy bee making the blossoms nod.

Jet plane fills the whole glen with noise. Keep walking.
The real spring is above and behind the little falls I found last time,

the water breaks from its hidden routes and spins and rustles out
and along, the rocks and pool almost aglow, rust-orange,

three women pass and the tiny pool fills and spills over time
and again and a speck of water sails all the way to my book

and blurs the word *pool* and a music like water begins within me,
not head or heart but all through, any reason will do, any bad excuse,

a music not for or from me but all those beings shaking
their dumb selves awake in here, what can I do, they are starting

to rub their eyes, to straighten up, where are we, do you remember,
Constantinople, the dread sea, some boggy farm, the hut along

the dirt road, what happened, fire, mud, stones, does it matter,
oh it's you! And she is here, too, and William, and the redbird,

how many of us are there, do we need to count, do we need to talk?
Should we lie down together or take hands and amble away?

Some of us want to listen, some to cup hands and drink
from the cold spring. Some of us think we should sing.

Ode to Luna with Implausible Quotations

She was nothing like a lover. She was my temptation,
my temporary obligation, draped on the soft chair or under

the plant stand on the deck, a cat so fat she was like
a soft bowling ball with fuzzy extremities, always asleep

or wanting to go out or come in. At night she yowled
every twenty minutes, just loud enough to wake me.

Fear is the parent of earthly love, she indicated,
and he who will not bend to love must be subdued by fear.

Fine, I said, and went out on the deck. She stayed in.
Back in the world, enormous firepower was not making

the enemies go away, but here in the deep shade it was
almost comfortable, splashes of light in the meadow,

birdsong in the trees. If song is the symptom, is there
a disease? *You are the child of great mistakes*, I heard,

and now you must learn differently. I waited and tried
to listen. *The great one is undivided,* sang the birds;

he lives totally in every living thing. Inside, Luna was
spraddled on the floor, asleep again. *When you are living*

honestly with someone, she breathed, *there are moments*
when God quietly enters the room. Tonight she sleeps on the deck.

February Report on Conditions in the Interior

1. I was either too early or too late again this morning, but the sun had me covered.

2. The tips of Scotch pine littering the backyard have stayed green for weeks. I still don't know if the wind or some demented squirrel took them down.

3. Last night the neighbor on the corner drove her old Buick up over the curb and parked on her own grass again.

4. Last week in Samarra, our guys drove their Humvee back to base with two dead insurgents strapped to the hood like deer.

5. The square of plywood nailed over the bottom half of the lime-green garage's broken window years ago is holding.

6. The three strange angels have not been seen in weeks.

7. No snow since December, and the ice shelves along the creek bank are shrinking and cracking.

8. Agonizing reappraisals of the true, the good, and the right continue.

9. Somebody sawed the big fallen limb into lengths just right for burning, then left them on the brown grass like a puzzle for dummies.

10. Everybody I know still showers completely naked. As far as I know.

11. *There is no one sleeping,* wrote Tony Hoagland.

12. I met him once in a diner in Baltimore, which is nowhere near Samarra.

13. *There is no one sleeping,* he wrote, *who does not dream of being touched.*

14. The leftover bale of straw is still at the edge of the garden, slowly and irreversibly becoming something else.

15. *A crucial dimension is one of humility,* wrote my smart friend.

16. *The gospels can be read as an anamnesis of blindness,* wrote his smart friend.

17. The president is threatening veto, but his minions are still restless.

18. The skaters are beautiful, strong, and angry.

19. Death said, "I was surprised to see your servant here in Baghdad, for tonight I must meet him in Samarra."

20. My eyes feel better since I've been using the lotion.

21. I can't lose those three Christmas pounds, though I've been riding the cursed bike every night.

22. Maybe tomorrow my heart will break out, or open, or down.

23. Maybe two riders are approaching and the wind will begin to howl.

24. Maybe my soul will grow so slender it can slip between sash and frame and enter the seamless blue.

25. A great golden dome was shattered yesterday in Samarra.

26. *Want to live forever?* the e-mail asks, but the message is empty.

27. Tonight we start to build another dome, in the secret place where the gospel is always clear and silent.

28. The ducks are still on the pond.

Where Water Finds an Edge
—Blue Hen Falls, June 2004

Nothing like a careful, thorough plan with one large error.
Too dark under the trees, too many roots—

we must turn back. Rocks piled around like bad excuses,
like my father's brow as he gently explains

just how deep and wide my screwup is. I stumble
for a place to sit, break through a thin sheet of shale.

Even the skin of the earth can't be trusted.
Every splash is a sign; not one is a word.

But we know the light was hiding all these stars.
We need the dark because it makes us clumsy,

because it makes us forget the banks
we are rushing between, muttering about hymns

and women while the falls spill out before us.
We will not need to be ready to tumble down.

We will shine and shout, and all the damage
will be forgotten soon. The water is not wounded

by its breathless journey, it bears its troubles lightly,
it does not falter as the full night arrives.

And the hard ledges glow, long after all else is lost.

Firefly

I want to find the room where my father is sleeping,
take his hand and wake him. I will say I am sorry

to have come so late, after all the other children.
I will ask about his heart and his dreams,

apologize for disturbing his rest. I want to drive there
faster than anybody, but I am not even on the way home.

The masters say all is one, but I am five hundred miles away,
studying the alphabet of broken trees

and the gorgeous dusk of the beaver marsh.
The masters say nothing is separate, but I am lost

among the lilies, the needly mosquitoes, the slow tenderness
of the fireflies. I will leave tomorrow if need be.

Tonight I will dream of the great healing,
and the night will be warm with the hum of fireflies,

the chir and splish of the beavers fitting one more stick,
one more slap of mud into the mile-long dam.

When Madonna Met Menno

"You're a slut," he said, "but God loves you anyway."
She took a long pull on her beer. "Don't be simple,"
she said. "I was a Catholic schoolgirl. I've known that
since I was twelve." She was all knees and ankles,

and he was a river toad, the two of them crammed
into a tiny booth among the hard-drinking yuppies.
"Besides, I've got babies now," she said, "and all that
whore stuff was for sales anyway." "I know what you mean,"

said Menno. "Most of my whoring was for the Church,
but I think I gave it up too soon." He took an even
longer pull on his beer. "I did a lot of brooding
about the Blessed Mary back then," he said. "I decided

that Jesus slid out of her like a seed through a tube.
She was just a vase for the beautiful flower." "What a load,"
said Madonna. "Mary was Jesus, and he was her, too."
"Yeah, I've been wrong before," said Menno. "You want

a basket of fries, another beer?" They could feel the subway
underneath them, a heavy snake hauling another wave
of puzzled souls from there to elsewhere. "No," she said,
"the kids will be home. Time to cross the river."

Letter with Melody and Fall from Chair

There is so much to explain. First I was one of those farm boys
with the hard and horny hands, the ones the farm girls feared

and disdained. For years, I tried to stay on nodding terms
with the people I used to be. Then I walked out of the temple,

and my guide discoursed upon the elephant, its mighty tusks,
its shoulders like boulders. But no, that wasn't me.

Like a dream, this world is best recorded the minute we wake up.
The strong woman said, *The I is a dark bar, a shadow on the page.*

She said, *Style is all a matter of rhythm, which makes a shape
in the mind.* Then she said, W*ell, I'm going,* and I let her walk.

When the verse ended, the fiddle picked up the melody,
and what I knew seemed a fog that was just about to clear.

Is anything more authentic than feeling like an imposter?
Most facts can be worried into fiction. The two old men said,

How dare you travel on your own? and just to say something,
I said, *God will protect me.* My wife and I drove around Haarlem

for a baffled hour before we figured out that our map had south
at the top. He said, *What the reader wants is an unbroken dream,*

and I fell off the chair. It's like *Fight Club:* no rules,
months of concrete and bruises, and it turns out

your mind has been beating up your face all the time.
Forget the notes and write to your unknown friends.

Forget about sitting, forget about travel. Wait for the music.
Fall out of your body. Another will be waiting.

The Song of the Weed Witch

> *No ideas but . . .*
> —William Carlos Williams

I could walk up or down the creek, but I stop. So little time.
Here's the strainer someone left on the rocks, the air
so damp it's one degree from fog. Here's the weed

rooted somehow in the mossy boulder, almost ready to seed.
Despite much instruction, I've never mastered the simple
clear explanation. I've never figured out how to put ideas

in things. In this simple, indescribably deep forest,
I remember last night when we were suddenly talking
about what might survive our bodies, and my new friend said,

I could go to church if I didn't have to believe all that stuff,
and I said I knew what she meant. But the beer was gone,
and we were tired. I got in the car, and the singer sang

Three crosses in a copse of trees, a long way from Calvary,
and I found my room, slept, woke into another
irrevocable and precious day and put not one idea

into a thing. I spoke mostly to the one inside who listens darkly
to my obnoxious supplementary monologues, the one
who says very little beyond *walk, then* and *sit here*

and *listen* and *wait*. There are many things--the mossy boulder,
a dead leaf sprawled on it, some wispy grass, lichens,
a foot-tall weed, almost ready to seed-- and not an idea

in the whole passel. Where the creek turns, a mist rose or lowered
or gathered. The whole forest spun without moving
and hummed without noise, simple and clear and enormous.

All these adjectives must die, I know, and be flung
on a heap like the honeysuckle that the weed witch is clearing
to let the natives flourish--skunk cabbage, spicebush,

jack-in-the-pulpit. I am a native but not exactly at home,
so I listened to the nearby water and the distant water,
and a drop fell on my shoulder like a reason to turn.

Report on Recent Activities in Austin (Selected)

I watched the bats boil distant and otherworldly from under the bridge

J discovered she'd booked the wrong flight and couldn't leave till
        Monday and left several wild messages on my cell phone

Later I left the stupid thing at airport security after noticing a dish
        full of pens and change somebody else had left behind and
        barely quashing the impulse to jam it all into my pocket

In between I walked among the tattoo parlors and T-shirt shops and
        empty bars in the hot quiet afternoon and then again late
        and dark, the streets jammed with young drunks and an
        enormous stretch Hummer, a door flung open, a woman in
        flowing dress crouched inside --*blow job,* I said, *I think she's
        throwing up,* J said, but we didn't stay to find out

And I laughed and ate and drank in the noisy rooms where my ears
        and soul were dented and bruised by all the good cheer and
        shameless butt-kissing, the way too much water from the
        hose will flatten the new tomatoes

We waited on the bridge as the sun glumly abandoned the city, not
        sure where to be or what to watch

I couldn't get the damn cell phone to ring, but when we finally
        found each other J told the story pluckily and we all told
        her how much fun she could have with a free day in the city

I walked her back to her hotel through the mostly happy drunks
        and some guy trashed on a bad powder tried to talk to us,
        Cheers, he said, and I turned away and thought we'd lost
        him but he followed, saying *Where are we? What is this?*
        until we walked away fast

J said, Wait, why did I ask *you* to walk me, you're such a pacifist, what are you going to do, ask to be beaten up and then burned at the stake?

So I made my standard promises and remembered hearing that war poetry was the fitting and proper genre for the humdrum brutality of America

And the bats swept out in a vast spidery ribbon of need and invisible sound, their hunger and delight carried them in skeins and pulls across the darkening sky, a huge scarf loosely knitted of fur and bones and sharp small teeth

And even in their numberless numbers they covered only a small arc of the sky, which accepted their passage with neither hunger nor delight

Lunch Poem at Snow Road

We say God and the imagination are one...
—Wallace Stevens

The hummers don't even care
when I come out through the door.

And those high wisps of cloud head north
as if they had an appointment

as two hawks swoop in the meadow
and are gone. And because it's lunch time,

I can say anything. Imagine my wife
walking home to eat, crossing

the hot streets of our town,
choosing the shade when she can.

Her headache's better today,
I hope. Let her keep walking,

enter the house, riffle through the mail.
I can imagine anything today,

I can remember my very first day,
how spirit and body slid together

like two hands joining. I remember
the cool flame that washed

and fused them into one, as God
and the imagination might be one,

as the bee smacks hard
at the window and falls to the deck

and lies buzzing incredulously
until it finds its wings and flies off

and does it once more to be sure.

Contemplation with Ledges and Moon

What do the hollows in the stone promise?
Where the scratched names stop, the rock mutters

what it meant all along. Here, the grizzled red maple.
There, yellow beech clenched hard to the cliff side,

a tulip tree smooth forty feet up. Edges blur
in the half-light, and the swallows work higher

and higher, and the bats revel, stretching
their thin webs around what they need.

The mind is a rattly gourd, the ego, a black marble.
The soul is very light and large, a cloud of leaves

that froth and fade into the wood thrush's cry.
There is no soul without the shy veery,

the whiny bugs hunting our heat, the gravel
working its way out from sandstone.

The soul is not a language or a cat or a catapult.
It is a net without mesh, a sail knuckling and filling

among fireflies and gauzy leaves, flowing into
every valley, filling every breath and stone, spinning,

keening, rising, dusty heartwood, silken fog.
The broken path through trees made us stumble,

but we found the wide meadow at last
where the great golden moon lifted up

from the well of her sleep and sent down
more borrowed light than we needed

as we cried out and whispered on our way.

From the Screen Porch

Not early, except for me. Hummers buzzed and zoomed;
blue jays chattered. When the demon demanded
that Shiva surrender his wife, the god opened his third eye

and created a bigger demon. *Eat the small demon*, he said,
but after a long chase the small demon begged Shiva
to save him, and he relented. *You made me to devour*,

complained the big demon; *what shall I eat?* And Shiva:
Why not eat yourself? The demon did, from toes to chin,
until he could eat no more. *This is the face of glory,* Shiva said.

I shall set it at the door of the temple. All this glorious
greenery, entrancing and expensive, I wanted to dissolve
into it, but I pulled out the pencil and the student poems

and made earnest inscrutable notations as the coffee cooled.
Just on the other side of the screen, I felt the hummingbird's
dive and the other fleeing in fear. In the high spruce,

the jay jittered, flashed, and swooped. *This face
is the face of glory,* she said. What *do* the birds know?
I scrawled carefully in the margins, and around my words

the white plane of the page slid away, the floor tiles
cooled my feet, the air opened and wandered all directions.
Devour myself? Yes. But why stop? I want to eat the world,

hummers and high pines and jays and deep earth and all,
eat and eat until inside and out sizzle and fuse and the face
of glory shines like a star and the great door opens at last.

Spring Tractates

> *Past the houses - past the headlands -*
> *Into deep Eternity -*
> —Emily Dickinson, #76

I.

When it rains, it rains. When it rains and then fades
to a dismal drizzle, I walk to church anyway, clutch the umbrella

and pass under the blooming pear tree and across the street.
When I feel this greedy and restless I grumble and annoy

my wife even more than usual. I scribble while the choir labors
earnestly through the anthem, may the mind of Christ live in me,

Amen. My pastor says Jesus still walks among us. He says little.
He ate fish with the disciples at Emmaeus, touched their perfect bodies,

lit their minds. Why am I restless when I have a big house,
many rooms, many windows, many doors? Like my preacher,

I was a nervous boy, worried mostly about the wrong things,
which is a kind of comfort now. Yesterday I bought six used books,

bored with all my dreary devices, dreaming of some musty page
that would charge everything again. For three bucks, I got all

the poems of Emily Dickinson—six for each penny. I came home
and read *Exultation is the going / Of an inland soul to sea.* I read

Bred as we, among the mountains, / Can the sailor understand /
The divine intoxication / Of the first league out from land? I'm a long way

from water. Fifty days to Pentecost. Patience, my pastor says.

II.
Absence makes the heart grow fodder.

The toddler on the sidewalk has learned the harmonica's secret--
breathe in, blow out, every note is sweet.

Its second secret rests in the space between the breaths.

I can see so far and touch so little.

For a week after I fell on the bike,
I forgot the scrapes along one shin,
but today I remembered
and flaked off the scabs until one bled.

After two glorious weeks, it was cloudy all day.
Out east, one milk-blue skein where the clouds have loosened.

How many rich browns and tans and grays
in the flaking stump at the water's edge?

Absence makes the heartwood falter.

Ha.

III.
> *My soul - accused me - And I quailed*
> *As Tongues of Diamond had reviled*
> *All else accused me - and I smiled -*
> *My Soul - that Morning - was my Friend*
>   -#753

Out the front door, ratty Scotch pine, then the parking lot.
Side windows: spiderwebbed blacktop of the driveway,

then the gray neighbor house, A/C unit, pile of old brick
under the seedy stairway to the second floor. In back,

grass and yard violets and dandelions, bird feeders,
no birds this morning. All sunk in green and dismal

domesticity, or so says my diamond-tongued soul.
It trusts nothing in this world, believes stoutly

in this world, rests hard in this world.

IV.
Oh Emily, you found a way out of town
so strange and clever nobody could follow.

How did you do it?
The first league is astonishing,
but the water is wide, the sky is gray,
the compass wanders like a weary drunk.

It's been centuries, or years,
or all day.

Whose road is this?

V.
Ah, admit it, all this angst and melancholy is phony--
these last weeks I've been smug

as a grain-fed trout as the spring unfolded
like God's own fancy parasol.

Even now, real live horses canter down the bike path,
and how can I worry about the gray in my beard

or soaring Chinese oil consumption or even
the misery and rubble my tax dollars are buying

when the cardinals are showing off
and the mallard sprints toward the far shore

with its green head glowing
and all the hard work happening out of sight?

All over town, the lilacs pour out clouds of essence,
and any walk means passing through

a dozen fragrant little heavens.

VI.
High up, the new cottonwood leaves
shine like mirrors,

like the starling's purple helmet.
In this much sun, everything blazes,

even the water shines.
The black snake ripples upstream

as quiet and dark as pure space,
as a man's or a woman's hunger.

VII.
Once I tried to sleep on roots and gravel
high in some foothills,

a cold April and the last firewood
bleeding into ash.

An intricate song washed everything
like a black dry ocean,

and I heard every note
and remembered everyone I had failed and deserted.

And then my soul, or some soul,
curled itself around me

like the down bag I didn't own.
It didn't speak a word, but I listened--

and centuries or years or hours later,
a shape felt its way out of darkness, and another,

and between them I saw four smooth stones,
four steps I could take.

Contemplation at the Bar R Ranch

Both the owner and his daughter said we'd have to see the crosses,
so of course I tried to avoid them. But wandering aimlessly

after sublimity as I do on free afternoons, I followed a sign
that said "Baptismal" down a narrow way

and stepped carefully on rocks across the icy creek.
When I looked up, there they were, enormous,

big enough to crucify a pteranodon or a giraffe.
As I climbed the muddy path, some part of me said,

I have to safeguard my doubts, and another remembered
how the old picker said to Goodman, *I find*

the prettiest woman in the room and play every song for her.
Too edgy to eat, Salinger's Franny tried to pray

the Jesus prayer all the way through homecoming.
With the sun low behind the crosses, I could barely look.

Thin grass, lichens, rocks, and gravel lay low all around,
stunned by some brutal devotion not their own.

Three weeks to solstice. Faint thin birdsong.
So many trees, so many rocks, so many women

whose lives and bodies I will never touch.
The creek rippled on, Shasta glowed in the chilly haze,

a strand of spider silk glinted in and out of sight.
Breathe in: *This is paradise.* Breathe out: *I must go.*

"Night, the Astonishing . . ."

One star only, and all the trees looming, not my enemies
nor my friends. Hölderlin praises the night: "the stranger

to all that is human," "mournful and gleaming."
But this night is wet heat and the insects that crave

any blood the way I crave red wine and whiskey,
sweet words in a row, and whatever it is we call God.

Inside, the lights press against the window,
show the stove and shelves, the table with its bottles,

all these homely things shining and the night behind them.
Luna pads to the door, and I let her out. It's late.

I am not a cat or a soldier to be out in the dark,
not the farmer in his roaring combine, taking off the wheat

before it rains. I walked in the hot woods all day,
I read and hummed and muttered on the soul and the spirit,

but there is no more in me than one star might say:
that it fused and changed itself for centuries, consumed

its own being to cast something outward, that its hot light
sailed reckless as Lucifer through oceans of space

to wash up on this undreamed, dark, occupied island,
to be gathered and known, to be spoken among the trees.

The Other Side of Empire

(ca. 2009)

Translation

Patience and Panic are death's twin children. They live in Vienna,
in a rent-controlled flat thrown up fast after the war. Food

and the trains are expensive, but wine is cheap. They get by
on shady deals, scavenging, small translation jobs, and the kindness

of their many irregular friends. Every month one of them borrows
the rent money from the other. When they can't afford heat

they sit in the cafes till four, argue metaphysics, disaster and desire
in three languages. If a stranger joins in they switch sides,

just for fun. The empire collapses around them. Another rises.
Walking home near dawn, the smoky music of a three-hour argument

on positivism and the Anschluss ringing in their heads, they feel
as safe as anyone deserves to be. They believe it might go on.

Damp Ode

Life, friends, is boring. We must not say so.
                    —John Berryman, "Dream Song #14"

The poet in exile sits alone at a table for six, the only one
empty when he stepped into the room with his plate
and bottle of water. He eats some sort of ham loaf,

potato salad, shredded carrots, things he could point at.
There's no menu, just food of various sorts behind the glass counters,
most of it not labeled, and the women serving seem unaware

that there *are* languages other than German. He's not here
because he's poor. He's here because he's cheap, and he forgot
his lunch again, and his wife isn't answering her phone.

It's crowded with locals eating fast as he is, in pairs or alone,
and one stocky older man settled firmly behind a tall beer,
determined to make it last an hour if not two. *Go, go, go,*

says the poet's inner voice. The plate is bare. He's still hungry,
but his body wants to be elsewhere, even if it's out in the rain,
halfway up one of the little Salzburg mountains, lost in a cold mist.

Everyone in the room is quiet, though the voices and clatter
of cooks and servers seeps in warm and loud from the other room.
Go, go, said the bird.
                    I'll go, feeling like the third or fourth man,

walk in the chilly rain back to my drab office filled with clouds
and self-pity, wishing for two big mugs of black American coffee.
I'll buy two little bottles of schnapps on the way out

as the man before me did, climb the Nonnberg and drink
them both straight down in the graveyard by the chapel.
Yes, life is boring, here and everywhere, but why should we

say so, even today, when the morning ride through
the wet snow left me chilled and damp for hours, soggy pants
and glum shorts. I could have taken the bus, or taken

the umbrella and walked. The clouds swirl and billow
around the Untersberg like skirts, like smoke, like clouds,
like the foggy breath of time, and how can I ask for more?

Somewhere Near Defiance

(2014)

Somewhere Near Defiance

> *It's late but everything comes next.*
> —Naomi Shihab Nye, "Jerusalem"

1.
I live near Defiance, a white name pressed on an old place.
Mad Anthony Wayne's soldiers broke down the orchards

when the battle was theirs, and built a fort
where the Auglaize and Maumee Rivers meet.

Water will answer anything, the moon, the wind,
the mud. The rivers mingle and move on.

2.
Once I drove my little car right into the heart of the empire,
huddled with my friends to plot and complain. All over town

the poets and other malcontents were hiding in the open,
vowing to split the rocks and terrify the despots.

In the coffeehouse we tallied our losses and wondered how
to subvert the lyric *I* until the hot waitress grabbed the mike

to say that racism wasn't over yet. We clapped for her,
then wandered toward the Capitol, launched some ragged

words to each other and the wind. All right, you can
have *shock,* we told the adversary, but *awe* belongs to us.

3.
Walt Whitman thought his poems might stop the war.
When they did not he moved to Washington, took a day job

so he could go to the field hospitals, read to the wounded,
write letters for men with no arms or eyes. *I have been hurt*

but am mending well. Do not weep, I will find you one day.
I walked around for days, found no field hospitals,

lots of monuments. I passed the suited and booted,
shaggy and lame, proud and weary, and it seemed

that each of us carried a wound we were trying to hide.

4.
Meanwhile the drone pilots turn their Hellfires loose
from dark rooms in the suburbs, buy a 6-pack on the way home.

1200 veterans of the last good war die each day,
and the stools at the VFW stand like puzzled mushrooms.

5.
These days I wake up grateful that my heavy dreams are gone.
I snag the zipper of my coat, pull it free, and walk off

puzzling over slides and words and stratagems. Then I step
into a room and see a row of faces, hopeful and new

as red and yellow apples hanging in the orchards of Defiance.

6.
The dawn came brilliant to my quiet town,
sun in the junipers, a mourning dove on the wire.

Nothing that I do matters to the earth or the sky.

But I've stalled around too long—it's time for declarations,
time for floods. Time to put down the *Toledo Blade*

and take a very long walk. Time to say peace on terror,
peace on drugs, peace on Defiance.

Peace on Mad Anthony and his soldiers—gone so quiet now—
and the warriors they fought, and the fruit trees they tore.

The Auglaize and the Maumee join and drift on,
exchanging sticks and soil and bits of news.

We are in the earth already, and the earth in us.

Even from Defiance, nothing's more than half a world away.

Meditation with Wallet, Eyeglasses, and Little Riley Creek

> *"The weak force of God settles down below in the hidden interstices of being, insinuated into the obscure crevices . . . "*
> —John D. Caputo, *The Weakness of God*

Which card is it that will open the steel door?

I know that one card will take me anywhere, or almost, and another will tell the authorities they should let me on the plane.

The kingdom of God, says Caputo, is like a beautiful old poem whose author is completely unknown.

My glasses have tiny rainbow sparkles on each lens, spreading as I scrape at them. The anti-scratch coating is separating, the office worker says sweetly, sometimes that happens, sorry they are not under warranty, well it's been two years and I will have to ask the doctor, what if something has changed?

The idea of one true religion, Caputo says, makes no more sense than the idea of one true poem.

For the fourth day in a row the brown roar of the creek bears tons of topsoil and effluvia toward the ocean.

Is there one true creek?

God is a *weak* force, says Caputo, a call, an event, a voice. All the rest is rouged and painted theology, the invention of men wishing to be strong.

If I scrape the anti-scratch coating entirely away, will I see something new?

If God is great but not strong . . . I take a deep breath, let it out.

A wren in the pine tree, pecking at the new cones, visible only when it moves.

It leaves a branch quaking as it disappears.

Autobiography with *Blonde on Blonde*

The ragman drew circles on everything, but St. John dragged
his feet through them all, saying *In the beginning was the Word!*

until time shuddered like a bus with bad brakes and my dad
rubbed his face and sat down at the kitchen table, his farmer tan

glowing. It had been a windy day, and the brutal stench
of Hillman's hogs wafted through the screens. I whacked Kathy

on the back of the head just to hear her howl. It worked.
Then they drove me off to college, where I learned

that the not-yet has already happened, if you squint at it
just right. *I am, I said,* said Neil Diamond, and we had

to agree with that. Then the president explained that those
unwilling to kill for peace might once have been good people,

but godless communist drugs had made them into trolls
and orcs. We knew he was an idiot--we were elves and hobbits--

and decided to set off for Mordor to destroy the Ring
right after dinner. But somebody put on *Blonde on Blonde* again,

and it was just like the night to play tricks, and we could hardly
root out the fascist pigs while Louise and her lover were so entwined.

We walked down beside the dam instead, tried to lose ourselves
in the scant woods. I never got to Memphis or to Mobile.

The hard rain was already falling, but the sun still shone like glory
some of those afternoons, with classes over and the long night ahead

and water roaring down the spillway like the great I AM.

Interior Housekeeping

"The burning city of my sorrow . . ."
—William Stafford

My sorrow is not a city, and not burning. It is Railroad Street
in my town, so small it has only six houses, all facing

the tracks, three of them neat and clean, two in need
of paint and shingles, one so poor that nobody remembers

how to open the door, how long ago the gas was turned off,
what dwells and swells inside the dark refrigerator.

Maybe there's an old man in the bedroom upstairs,
drinking from the rusty sink tap, eating stale corn chips

and oreos. His wife left a note, but it fell behind the stove.
He took what he could find upstairs a week ago, knowing

this was his last trip. He pared mold off the last wedge
of cheese with a table knife, then tried it on his arm.

Twice he heard the phone ring, the second time for an hour.
He remembered to put the cat outside. He ripped the bag

of food right down, filled the water dish. He locked the doors.
The sheets have flowers on them. The blanket is wool.

A family of squirrels is living in the wall near the chimney.
They scratch and chitter all night. He scratches back.

No Path

Kayak on the quarry: will you hug the shore, push straight across,
waver or dawdle? No paths on the water. Almost November,

and the poison ivy is still green. The soft trap of sky closes
all around. An artful little spray of leaves near the shore,

as though Martha Stewart were sitting in for God.
Give up all that Father stuff, said Gordon, *look where it's got us.*

And the Warrior—even worse. The kayakers lift and dip
their paddles, orange signals: this way for us. So much is offered,

so much goes begging, and still what we need evades us, or hides
in plain sight. On the water, every way might be the right way.

God might be the Father and the Warrior and the lost leaves,
the water and the bleached trunk, motion and stone,

lush twists of cloud and barking dog and wind,
star upon star alert and invisible in every direction,

low moan in the blood, circle and drift in the bright cells,
shadowy hum and whir of electrons, fizz and buzz and shush

too small to name. No end, no opening, no tribe, no answer.
Only this: kayak and paddlers, lift and dip,

breath and muscle above the chill water, below the soft sky.

—for Gordon Kaufman

Having It All Four Ways

> *By a* primal *oneness the four--earth and sky, divinities and mortals— belong together in one.*
> —Heidegger, "Building Dwelling Thinking"
>
> *Now I a fourfold vision see . . .*
> —Blake

Prologue

Triangles are very strong, but groups of three are unstable.

As for two, when is that enough except in bed? Even in bed?

And one, oh, we can never be alone in this world, the universe bends and we twist, it shudders and we shake, the clouds of witnesses bloom like gnats along the springtime trails.

So why use so much ink, grumpy, unsatisfied? Here are the graceful and portentous branches, the dependable water, the ether and the stone.

When will we find purchase in this world, if not in the grace and balance of the eternal four?

Some Inexact Examples of the Four Elements

Sweat, chocolate, lust, and fire.

Wheat straw, columbine, saffron, and the magic mountain.

William Blake, Patty Griffin, John Coltrane, and Colombian Supremo French Roast.

Straw for the garden, a hoe worn thin by sharpening, the first radishes, and one of those old Oliver tractors with a narrow front end.

An old oak desk with new varnish, a corkscrew willow, the wind circling the room like a curious spirit, and the voice calling *Hey hon? you wanna start the grill?*

Now, whenever, should have, and maybe.

Catechism and Confession (Partial)

What have you read?
    Too much, not enough.

What have you seen?
    Not enough, too much.

What do you know?

Which of the sirens do you love?
    The noon siren, for it means we all are safe.

Which of the sirens do you love?
    The late night siren, for it means I am safe.

Which of the four stones do you love?
    The black granite, or the red. No, the limestone.
    No, the stone I cannot name.
    No.

Which do you love, mother or child?
    The mother, because she does not look at me,
    because she has forgotten she is beautiful,
    because she is wearing her spring shorts,
    because she cares only for the child.

Further Remarks

When the four elements have their mojo on, the fields tremble to be plowed

When the four elements are as instruments well in tune, the skies turn red though the sun is long gone

Where the four elements mingle in due proportion, there the old men startle upright in their limousines, tear up the secret agreements, disappear alone into the mountains

When the four elements speak in harmonious accord the boys and girls loiter around the swimming pool and saunter home the long way, towels hanging loose about their loins

When the four elements are truly named the spheres will lock and fuse and deliver us, the valleys be exalted and the rough places plain, the lion caress the lamb, the little streams of alcohol come trickling down the rocks

Where the number is four desire and beauty are two sides of the fourfold coin, inscribed along its edge and in its arc and spin, glinting on every surface, and in the watcher and the one who tosses, and the coin falls through the quivering air to the shimmering stone

When the number is four the naming will begin, names for the none, the many, the lost hidden squandered obliterated, the annihilated ridiculed scraped into plastic and dumped in the landfill, yes the names are difficult

Where number is four the great eye and its circles the ear and the voice sway and tremble into speech into silence into music into flesh

Meditation with Muddy Woods and Swinging Bridge

[The covenant] is structured in violence and steeped in blood, from the blood of circumcision and endless animal slaughter to brutal extermination of the 'people of the land.'
—Grace Jantzen, *Violence to Eternity*

Hot wind from the west. Trail still soft after a whole week's drying.

Deer tracks, coon, one stubborn mud-hiker's deep scours, each like a little boat or a long wet nest.

Wood piled everywhere--neat rows for woodstoves, heaps of trash and branches.

We were in Salzburg when a great storm scattered the old trees on the Kapuzinerberg like pickup sticks.

Today I brought nothing but pens, keys, comb, notebook, bicycle, lock, wallet and credit cards.

And knees a big black fly seems to like, and shorts with a pocket ripped two summers ago, still not fixed.

Morning reading: What kind of God would drown every living thing that wouldn't fit on some puny ark? Would slaughter the people of Canaan for the sake of one hungry band of nomads?

Many good gravel paths lead from the subdivision into the woods, but only the animals use them.

Somebody's cutting something hard in a dry swimming pool.

Who discovered we could cast our anger at the sky and get it back named God?

In my old house the bathroom sink plugs up every four months but I know exactly how to swear and clear it.

Small white blooms all over the multiflora rose, bushes twice my size.

Seed pods float in the pond like mothers determined to tan whether or not their children get lost in the bushes.

On a day this hot and green it seems crazy to think that God picks sides.

One plank of the swinging bridge is missing, one bowed and soft, and a big lost branch is wedged high between the end posts, but I walk across it anyway.

Slippers

I used to believe I could be a crow, or a pheasant running
long-tailed and pretty down the rows of broken stalks,

oblivious of shotguns. I used to believe in spontaneous rebirth,
in the multiplicity of rewards, in the indefinite renewal

of overdue books. I used to dream of the wearying privilege
of travel, the miraculous beauty tapping at the motel door

at 2 a.m., saying *It's Angel.* I used to believe that each step
was easy, and that I could recover from any fall. I used to run

and never get tired in the humid summer dusk, playing horses
with my cousins at somebody's birthday party, through

the ditch lilies and the high grass. I did not believe then
that every step contained a fall. I had never watched a man

work his way slowly from wheelchair to car seat, his shirt
and pale belly spilling out. I would never have thought

the snow would pile this deep, would last this long, that I would
walk the icy narrow paths looking down, leaning forward,

careful as any man who has fallen more than once,
any man thinking of his Christmas slippers and soft chair

just a hundred steps away, a dozen. I used to believe
that every step was too slow, that I would run faster next year,

that I would rise up stronger each time I fell, spitting out
the mouthpiece, my whole body singing from the stranger's

helmet, from the stranger's body breaking over mine.

On the Birthday of Ronald Reagan and My Mother-in-Law, I Mourn Jerry Garcia

Water loose, raw and smelly all over town again, nearly as much as the last big flood, then it turned sharp and snowed a little and I frittered away the day finding clips from Youtube to reinforce my bitter lectures on the Cold War.

I walked home, switched computers, browsed and brooded some more, found Jerry Garcia plump and old in cut-off shorts, singing a heartbreaking "Peggy-O."

For a moment I rested in the old dream that sad lovely songs on the folly of war will make us stop killing each other.

Will you marry me, pretty Peggy-O? If you will marry me, I'll set your cities free . . . Jerry's gray hair blows in the wind. He looks nearly dead, and he is.

Reagan insisted that once the Russians knuckled under and found Jesus we could all be pals.

My mother-in-law, still living in blurry and complicated comfort in a condo in Surrey, BC, resembles him in ways that shall not be detailed here.

The snow stopped, and the streets began to freeze.

If ever I return, pretty Peggy-O . . . If ever I return, your cities I must burn, and destroy all the ladies in the aree-o.

Reagan led the so-called free world well after his dementia had begun to show. The Dead played thousands of shows. Jerry did not live a pure life.

After the somber, shimmery guitar solo, one more verse: *Sweet William, he is dead . . . and buried in the Lousiana country-o.*

And then our neighbors' blind basset hound Herald stepped out, and proclaimed the need for attention to small things moving in the soggy chilly night.

The Unreliable Narrator Remembers the Martyrs Mirror Conference

I. Preliminary Remarks

The full title: *The Bloody Theater or Martyrs Mirror of the Defenseless Christians Who Baptised Only Upon Confession of Faith, and Who Suffered and Died for the Testimony of Jesus, Their Saviour, From the Time of Christ to the Year A. D. 1660,* makes everything plain, if not simple.

In 1660 the author and Dutch churchman Thieleman J. Van Braght was asked to answer for the boldness of his stance. He had stood firm against the Collegiants, who baptized durn near anybody and let sinners take communion, who said the True Church was not only invisible but nowhere existed upon this earth.

His vast book asserted that the True Church remains "visible, discernible, and distinguished from other nations," that a golden thread runs from the Lord Jesus Christ through the defenseless martyrs of all ages, tormented, burned, pressed hard by the many false Christians. The errors, sins, and horrors of "the ungodly and false church" are documented in fifteen large pages, under headings like "Two, Three, and Four Popes Reigning at the Same Time."

These are sad and dangerous times, Van Braght said, when Satan comes among the quiet and comfortable in the twilight, in a strange yet pleasing form, when the world reveals itself very beautiful and glorious, pleasing to the lust of the flesh and the eye. Mighty buildings, garments from abroad, great dinners with no thought for the poor.

It sometimes seems to us, he said, *as if heaven had come down upon earth, or that we were ascending from earth to heaven. . . . We walk no longer upon earth with our thoughts; nevertheless, we are still encompassed by a cloud of earth, a body of clay, a heavy load of the soul.*

II. Miscellaneous Facts and Assertions

To make Van Braght's list, a martyr need only have been defenseless, a believer in adult baptism, and of course a Christian.
The Ephrata *Martyrs Mirror* of 1748 was the largest printing project of colonial America.
A million large sheets of paper were handmade and printed.
Leftover pages were confiscated for musket wadding in the Revolution, and so the book became a body, torn and shredded, burned in its turn.
The recent English edition, with its grocery-sack cover and red-splattered end pages, is far too large to read in bed.
When the body is burned its ash becomes words, its freed atoms become story.
In the Catholic martyrology, innocent priests are murdered by hideous mobs, the cathedrals desecrated, the holy relics smashed and plundered.
If the stories of wounds do not ring true for you, perhaps you have not been sufficiently wounded.
A book needs to be touched, like a child or a silk sheet, like a handful of raspberries, like a loaf of bread.

III. Questions for Discussion

Explain a) the relation between martyrdom and selflessness and b) the need for a crowd of onlookers.
How can one be sure that the Holy Spirit has guided the act of translation?
What language did Adam speak, and how might it be recovered?

"The self is nothing but a shifting concatenation of errors, flaws, and blunders." Discuss.

Compare and contrast: the martyr, the athlete, the gladiator.

If the book of a thousand stories has collapsed into the image of Dirk Willems turning back to pull his pursuer from the icy pond, what then?

What if the *Mirror* reflected something other, something more, than death? What new, bright, stunning life might we glimpse among its myriad stories, its clouds of witnesses, its parade of fools and heroes, innocents and earnest explainers, its flames and blood?

What if we all are children left to hold a pear, or a twisted bit of metal, or the fading scent of the flesh that bore us into this world, caught for a moment more in our own fleeting bodies?

Contemplation with Rainy Birdsong

1.
When it stops raining, the loons will barely notice.
When it stops raining I'll push down my hood.

When the rain stops maybe I'll remember
that the fight in the heart is not to complain

unless it's really someone's fault, to notice
the line made by water dripping from the rope

that holds up the tarp that keeps us sort of dry.

2.
The rain will stop and we'll wish it would rain.
It will rain again when we don't want rain

and I'll walk with my sweetie and just as I am
thinking how beautiful she is she will complain

about her hair frizzing everywhere, and I will say
that it foams around her face like an angel's.

3.
When it rains the low camp bird will come out unhappy
to search among the roots and stones,

and the white-throated sparrow whose song
is common as air in these trees will sing it

like it's never been heard before
and will be lost forever when he lets it go.

Contemplation on Rules and Lines

One law for lion and ox is oppression, but of which one?

The ghost of Wm. Blake, gnarled and smiling in the hollow between tree and stone, refuses to say.

One law for water and rock is precision. Whenever they meet, water does all the talking.

Another law is rubbing. Another can be spoken clearly only in loon. Another takes 300 Earth years to state in full.

A lost fishline dangles like a strand of the golden thread, left behind by a traveler who went back home with nothing but bug bites and a solid case of jock itch.

I'm not so careful myself but I wish I were, and I tell myself that counts for something.

The wind's law is this: be yourself, and I will show you what that is.

The water's law is this: Tell me anything. Only my face will answer. I will hold the little ones in their little boats, I will let them go where they choose if they have the strength.

I will tell them what they must know, even if it breaks their backs or their hearts.

I will tell them what they want to know only if they ask very softly, and more than once.

Contemplation on Rain and Religion

I've decided that I'm religious but not spiritual.
—Gregory Wolfe

I always feel more religious in the sunshine,
especially if it's not hot and the place is pretty

and most people can't afford to get there or just
don't bother. Morning has broken and all that.

And so the rattle of rain on the tarp doesn't really
make me count my blessings, the stray drops

beading my borrowed rain pants don't bring
me bliss, the fact of fewer mosquitoes

than yesterday does not make my heart leap up.
But I know this: one day I must learn

to give up for good on getting dry,
to love the hiss of water falling into water,

the gray lake meeting the gray rain,
so little between them, our slender place

between the great sky and the stones.
Hold tight, I tell my heart, here we go.

Something the Winter Wren Didn't Say

Any place to sit will do because I aim to disobey,
to disappear, to wait and listen till the hard earth

shudders open like a touch-me-not. Rocks
like spilled treasure waiting for the dragon,

like junker cars rolled downhill toward the crusher,
like science waiting for fiction. Whose idea was it

anyway, to wait so long, to let all this accumulate?
The tanager and the winter wren both want to sleep,

but neither is willing to give up the last word.
I'm more like the rocks—I've slept for centuries.

But I remember now: after a hundred good nights
our lover the moon got bored and nudged

this corner down, roughed things up to mark
her place just in case, and went away.

She hasn't come close to us since. We made
many low songs almost as sweet as the wren's

and the tanager's, desperate to lure her back,
but we see her roaming through the wild sky

and know she's seeing that bully sun,
letting him drive his hot car a million miles an hour

with no seat belt, parking in a black hole
and spreading wide for him, riding him till

she glows so white and wet the world cracks and bellows,
and the rain pours down to turn our rage to tears.

Evening with Long Books

*Each man is a half-open door
leading to a room for everyone.*
　　　　—Tomas Tranströmer

My friends say Tolstoy really got into the heads
of his female characters. They give him credit.
They talk dreamily of the books they love,

books so long only two will make a whole course.
This seems to me like making twelve gallons of chili
and eating nothing else till it's gone, but I smile

and listen. My friends are smarter than me
and more patient, surely. I'm the only guy
in the house tonight so I get my own room

with a good foam mattress, a bad desk, windows
that open on other rooms. I make up the bed
and lie down with Tranströmer's poems,

ten or twenty lines on a page, fewer words
in fifty years than Tolstoy or George Eliot put down
in a decent work week. *Every man is a half-open door.*

The door to my room is cracked open,
lights blaze outside. My friends are all upstairs.
If I don't shut the light off, no one will.

The wind will settle toward morning, the waves
begin again to spell their single complicated word.
Waiting for the ferry we watched a hawk

try to lift a four-foot snake from the shallows,
drop it, circle, swoop and grab again and lose
its grip and veer away. Oh, how sweet would

that meat have been, how grand a feast, how we
would have cracked and sucked the bones,
how long we could have made that story last.

Oh

> *And you say Oh, then* Oh!
>   —Keith Ratzlaff, "Ending in Oh"

Rocks like Jeffers described: hard headed, stiff witted,
but not chatterers or fools. Not easy to walk on them,

but not dull either. East, the mainland is lost in murk
and haze. West, the last sun tints a few tentative clouds.

Yesterday I read Robert Hass's account of the difference
between "Oh" and "O," which was offered with complete

confidence and matched my own views not at all.
The heat is supposed to break tomorrow. A family

of otters prowls just offshore, diving for dinner, staying close.
The low thrum of the freighters never quite stops.

How many steps between vast calm and total panic?
When I say "Oh" I mean "O," if Bob Hass is around.

If Ratzlaff is around, I don't know what I mean.
I couldn't hear the freighters at first, and now

I can't stop listening. This long rock, like an enormous
baguette gone stale. Like a fossil finger pointed

toward Bellingham or Blaine or Mt. Baker. Like
the colored pencil God threw down when it was time

to quit on the shore line and make some seals and gulls
and crabs. And now the cloud bank over White Rock

has burst into color—another few miles is nothing for the sun—
and the little people-lights hug the skin of the world

like God knows what, like fireflies or deer eyes
on the road, like embers of a fire left to burn out

on a windy afternoon, no rain for weeks, the forest
so dry, oh, the arbutus leaves rustling, Oh, O.

—For Keith

Notes from the Faculty Meeting

After eight years of bounty, the cow has dried up.

Behind the great man the shield icon pulsed, patient as a heart.

Like seeds, some ideas appear whole and undamaged
but will never sprout.

Any form of motion draws the eye.

So far, every page of this yellow pad has torn ragged.

This troubles me more than it should.

I vowed to hold my breath until I heard a concrete noun.

Does "things" count? "Students?" "Projections?"

My attempt at narrative, jumbled already, was interrupted
by the need to applaud.

The phrase "difficult challenge" was not followed
by showers of gold.

"Forming a task force" did not lead to "pursue the Great One."

Most students believe they're more honest than most students.

After a national search, we hired Randy's brother.

Additional Assertions on Soul

Only moving does it have a soul.
—Pablo Neruda, "Ode to Bicycles"

1) All stones, even those from the moon, must share a single soul.

2) Dragonflies each have the soul of another, and spend their lives chasing their own.

3) Barns have souls until the main timber breaks.

4) Birds have souls only when singing, flying, or at rest.

5) Butterflies are so light because they abandon their souls at birth.

6) Automobiles have souls made of grease and fire, just like us.

7) The heron's soul is all bone and feathers, an excellent mother despite its lack of hands and breasts.

8) The tiger lily's flower is tender and sweet on the tongue, and its soul likewise.

9) We believe the earth has a soul, but nobody has ever gotten its attention.

10) The many tiny souls of the grass were at perfect ease until Whitman began to ask questions.

11) The air is one wild soul looking blindly for the lost one.

12) And the water, oh it carries many souls, but keeps none for itself.

On the Way to the Glacier

I.
The ocean said: it's simple, but will take years to explain.
The mountain said: never mind, you'll never get it anyway.

We took the train despite the old ones' warnings, creaked up
the coast range and rolled through the high, soggy valley

where the leaning peaks wore their fog caps all day long.
The fjord wind kept changing its view of all the tough issues,

the brilliant sun explained everything in one long sentence,
and we didn't nod off even in the drowsy afternoon.

When we left the train we forgot it all at once, and the clouds
rolled over like the capes the on-board magicians use

when they're not demanding applause or displaying their torsos,
and the thin streak of light that leaked in from the north said,

stay awake, don't falter, be ready to take to the boats.

II.
So I faced back like the Angel of History while you read
and the old ones rested. We knew we must cherish them

even when they forgot the directions, complained of obscure pains
and refused to get off the ship. We saw them to bed and walked

on the wild top deck where the sun loitered until 10:30.
The horizon was a perfect seam for the eye to follow,

searching for the manic portal. The ship never faltered
and the world opened easily and slid shut behind us,

over and over. I drank coffee on the fantail and scowled at anyone
who approached, the staff did not try to comfort me, the breeze

took my cup when it was empty, the wreckage of our passage
spilled out behind, all foam and desolation too deep to reckon.

And somewhere forward the old ones dreamed of their courtship,
how he sang "Goodnight Irene" for her in Yarrow, and then

woke to wonder when they'd promised to meet us for dinner.

III.

And down one deck the wind was only a rumor and the banks
rushed by on all sides, steep as a hasty marriage, and on the ridge line

trees pointed like spears or signals or the last row of the crowd.
We came in fast and left the same way, touched almost nothing,

washed our hands often with soap and water. We ordered
everything on the menu and our waiter pleased the children

with his napkin tricks, the shoe, the mouse, the rose. It's good
to serve, and to make a thing into another. His children study

in Manila with the money he sends back. He was below decks,
off duty, when we stopped to watch the glacier calve,

its music slow and deep as any great fall. *I remember*,
said the guide who came onboard to explain this to us,

when I was young, I slept on the island in the seal camp,
and all night each night the white thunder filled our sleep.

Meditation in Glen Park with Springs and Bad News

We are in and of the world, materially embedded in the same
rain-drenched field that the rocks and the ravens inhabit . . . .
All our knowledge, in this sense, is carnal knowledge.
   —David Abram, *Becoming Animal*

Season of white butterflies, common, light and lovely.
Of beech trees split at the ground so that they might

almost be men, almost be women. I ran here, then walked,
then finally sat still. Trickle of water, whisper of wind,

creak of distant bird, slope full of hemlocks--not
soldiers but protectors, not heroes but guardians.

When we sat at the springs Karen said *this is a thin spot*
and I knew what she meant but asked her to explain.

I tried to talk about my summer reading, that I had learned
again that the world is alive, all of it, and full of sense,

but the words rang so thin and feeble that I stopped,
and we sat in the green shade and worried uselessly

about her new bad news. And the cold water rose
through sand, blinked in the beads of sun that sifted

through leaves, went quiet, obedient and perfect
on its way. Once every story had its place, Abram says,

place was mnemonic to the story. I can say only bits
and pieces from this place, high clouds, black squirrel,

ovenbird, dark sand wet across the valley's crease,
clear trickle easing toward the lake. I moved within it all,

neither welcome nor foreign except as I chose, an animal
among the animals, a creature neither great nor small.

In a clearing where a great tree had broken four others,
I thought suddenly that Wallace Stevens asked the right

questions but got the answers wrong. The new bridge
gleamed with its raw lumber, and the idea of a necessary

fiction seemed absurd. I sat down where the water
was loudest and admired the rough bench, the old dark tiles

that hold the springs until they overflow. These seemed
the necessary constructions, even if no one was there

but me and the butterflies. *I want you to write this place,*
Karen said, *I want to see it in a poem.* Yesterday the doctors

poked G. for the biopsy, tomorrow it's the Cleveland Clinic.
She will not sleep well. Death is not the mother of beauty.

It is its dusty mirror, the crease in the ravine where
the water must run. The white butterfly found a flower,

folded its wings to drink. I bent to the spring, dipped
my hands, cooled my face and sipped and walked away.

The Traveler Ponders Some Rumors

(ca. 2016)

The Traveler Ponders Some Rumors
That Have Reached His Ears

He's heard stories of amber, of winter storms that deposit
yellow knurls and knuckles the length of the long beach

that runs north to Palanga, of roads jammed even in winter
on a fair Sunday with beachcombers eager for treasure.

He's not found that road yet, shy or distracted or put off
by some vague sense that the old powers should be

cautiously approached. He's read that the Christians found
this land hard to enter, the people stubborn, claiming

to be happy with the gods they knew. That's been centuries.
Still the borders mean something. Still the news is bloody

and not so far away. The traveler read in the U. S. news
that there's new word from Vilnius: if the Russians come,

stay calm. Show up for work. Hug your children. The traveler
has noticed nothing scary, but he knows he's wearing

a snug cocoon of ignorance. Anyway another source insisted
that the message was mostly about storms, fire, earthquakes,

the Russians only one of many perils that need forethought
but not fear. He doesn't know whether the bundled souls

he passes on his night walks are brooding on blood, or thinking
only of their doors and dinner and a drink, or wondering

how much amber the last storm of winter washed up
on the beach, how much waits half-buried to give itself

to any walker, golden as cool fragments of a lost sun.

Windy Walk with Espresso and Globalization

"I have forgotten my mask, and my face was in it."
-Kenneth Patchen, *The Journal of Albion Moonlight*

In the coffee shop on the second floor of the mall with the big Iki
grocery, the traveler read on his phone that maybe Dylan read Patchen

in the sixties. The music, raucous, is "I work my ass off." The clerk
just said "one" to him, so he furrowed his brow. His espresso

was one euro, she meant. Absurd. With a glass of water and a little tray,
in a cup that says *il Pellino del caffè*. His face and mask are quite in place,

plenty of euros holding them up. Despite his ignorance of the language,
he can get anything he needs as long as he only needs things.

A former student wrote, *You're so close to Poland now, come and see us!*
The Soviet apartments are ugly but the women are beautiful,

the girls too. There's Carlsberg on tap—six months ago he drank it
with his son in China. The wind outside is not cold but still brutal,

it blew over a dumpster by the old apartments, he hefted it but
no way could he lift it. There's golf from South Africa on TV,

Fitzpatrick in third place is -9 and just hit a fine approach. There's
Jägermeister, Johnny Walker Red. The blond girl scampers up

the aisle and back to her mother, who feeds her a bite. *There is
at most one world*, said somebody. The girl runs up the aisle

and back to her mother, accepts another bite, drinks Coke
through a straw as her mother steadies the glass, runs again,

nearly crashes into the waitress. A man says something quiet
to the other waitress as he pays. She smiles with her whole face

as she clears his table, sits to eat her own lunch, leans
to whisper to the other waitress. There is at least one world.

Windy Walk with Hooded Crows

This northern life must be two, no three, of those black-headed,
gray-bodied birds. They *look* like crows, they stalk the forests

stubborn as partisans who know they will die for a lost cause,
who list the code names of their fallen comrades, who sit

in miserable bunkers and write *What if nobody wanted to sacrifice?*
and *Spring is coming but not to Lithuania.* So wrote Lionginas

Baliukevičius, aka Dzūkas, in 1949. *I sit and think*, he wrote,
but my thoughts don't materialize into anything. The birds *are* crows,

hooded crows, similar to the carrion crow but elevated to full
species status in 2002. The partisan Dzūkas died in 1949,

his country not free, his last hideout collapsed. The traveler skipped
to the end of the brave, sad journal, a few sentences in praise

of Tolstoy, who went pacifist and ate no meat in his last years,
who wrote *All, everything that I understand, I understand only*

because I love and *The two most powerful warriors are patience*
and time. The crows live in the forest, walk its enigmatic floor,

test everything they find. Love nothing. Stay away from the bunkers.

Things Overheard, Observed, and Possibly Misunderstood

1. The word for frost in the trees is something like *scarŝna,* certainly not spelled that way but surely beautiful even against the gloomy brick of the large blocks of flats, even against the heavy skies and the great smokestack emptying masses of gray smudge into the wintry air.

2. Only the dog across the street who is angry with every aspect of his life could be angry on such a morning.

3. He has distilled this displeasure into a poem of a single syllable, which he loves so much he repeats it several dozen times an hour.

4. People tend to do things you don't want them to do, she said. You want to convince the machine to do everything it can for you.

5. "We are like an artist who is frightened by his own drawing of a ghost," said Thich Nhat Hanh.

6. The sea was so calm yesterday, she said, I could have walked on water.

7. Did you try? asked her friend.

8. After dinner we walked to the Rimi for cash, cheese, chocolate, cinnamon. We took the shortcut through the quiet neighborhood, though one stretch is muddy with construction.

9. A young man saw us scrabbling around in the cheese section and said in English, Can I tell you something? You should try this one, it is our country's cheese, it is delicious, you will not be sorry. We took it home—it was hard and yellow, fragrant and earthy and yes, delicious.

10. I tried to say *scarŝna* before class, and my students hooted and snorted. They said it, I tried again, and they hooted again, louder.

11. We are building rapport and learning to appreciate our cultural differences.

12. A major difference is that the students switch among their various languages constantly, they laugh and joke and exchange deep confidences with each other as though Babel never happened.

13. I feel like I'm riding a unicycle in a land of four-wheelers.
14. Or like a ninety pound man with one huge bicep.
15. Yet they don't seem to care, they tolerate my jokes, they ask me questions: *borrowed words*, is that the right term?
16. All words are borrowed, I think later, who do we get them from, how will we ever pay back what we owe?

The Indolent Professor Is Shamed
into Uncertain Epiphany

I thought I'd put an easy little poem into the pile, a silly bar dream
with odd numbers on the bills, third-rate quasi-Kafka. Then I read

the first two student poems, and they were full of awful beauty,
chapped mouths to the side of the head, best friends shot

through the eye. Then John dropped by and told me how once
he re-filed the tumblers on the gas cap lock of his old Volvo to fit

the key, while laid up with mono. It wasn't hard, he said. I know
maybe two other people who would have even tried. I looked again

at my scrawly little notes. Then I looked out the window, drank
the thick mess at the bottom of my cup. Then perhaps on the steps

outside three lovely women slipped off their dark coats, shook out
their wings, cried once and flew away. Then it could be that the man

who cleans the grounds took out his little broom and swept it up
and down and the sky went entirely strange and a wash of some

un-nameable color spread over every stodgy red block of flats and
dingy car and dirty street, every tired woman with two Iki bags,

every bleary-eyed and silent man. And the crack at the edge of the sky
is where the light enters, brilliant but not blinding, as if to undo

the last bitter century and the six before, bombs and boots and bullets,
cattle cars full of people, all the rest. The light slid over the world

as if to shield its many good people from the current catastrophes
and all senseless pain to come, gently and with no need for vengeance,

to lift all misery and fling it into the sun. And I remembered
yesterday, the snow billowing as we walked to the Rimi, hunched

and slumped like refugees but snug in our good coats and boots,
knowing we would be warm soon, the wind mostly at our backs,

money in our pockets for bread and cheese and anything we needed.
And we met two girls on the sidewalk, the snow pelting them

so they had turned to walk backwards. When they heard us they
turned again, wincing, to face the icy pellets. And yet even as they

moaned and wailed into the storm they were laughing too.

Palanga Stintas

And in Palanga today one can find smelts baked or smoked,
dried, singing, dancing, metal, molar and amber, or tasty

fish soup, for today is Palanga Stintas and the little fish
give themselves up unwillingly but in great numbers

and the good people dress in their winter finery and walk
all the way down Basanavičiaus Gatveje to the great

L-shaped pier, crowded like hens in a run or fish in
a weir, the young and the old, lovers and grim couples

and somewhat happy families and pairs of girls
almost too young to be on their own. We all walk

between the fish stands and the vendors selling fur hats
and amber necklaces and cups and pots and soup

and karšas vynas, the warmed red wine, and Svyturas
in big glasses, eight black coats and then a blue one,

eight more and a yellow, nine more and a sudden pink,
strollers with weary toddlers moaning and women

bearing inscrutable small dogs, all of us walking
together and apart, bumping and jostling, up the slope

of the barrier dune and down to the sea at last,
out along the beach where the dogs can run free,

out along the pier where the crowd thins at last,
where the long-haired women pose for their men

over and over, the obscure sea behind them,
the women smile and remember how beautiful

they are even in winter, even in their black tights
and black coats zipped high against the wind.

The Traveler Attends the Friday Evening Concert

("Katarsiai ir Kataklizmai," Petras Geniušas, fortepijonas, at the Klaipėdos Koncertų Salé, 2015 m. vasario 27 d.)

If the traveler was a detective he would decipher everything,
he would read every word in the city's book, he would know

every cognate and *faux amis* and never confuse them. Sometimes
a shiny black Steinway is just a piano. He wants to see

the smooth brick walks for the breakable gift they are, the sturdy
concrete of the new footbridge, the streetlights arcing on.

He would understand why the small dogs must wear sweaters,
even when the evening is soft. He would be grateful

for the rocky path that cuts the angle to the bus stop,
even if the stones make his ankles ache. And when he entered

the hall he would not need to be told how rare and fine it is
to sit in comfort in the red seats, to merely turn his legs

to let the woman in her fine dress pass, to pay a paltry nine euros
for the seventh seat in the seventh row, to hear the pianist

whose name is almost genius, who bears his gift so modestly
that the whirl of sound seems a discovery from behind or below

or within him, so that the traveler's first thought is *splinters
from*—but no, there is nothing broken. Sparks, perhaps,

from the great wheel where a sword of no earthly metal
is sharpened. But no, there is no weapon here. Flickers

of a new light, perhaps, an old light, something carried silent
in the heart and bones and fingers for centuries, in the soft brain

and the wispy nerves. *Catharsis or Cataclysm.* What will
it be? The red buildings where the Russian troops bunked

are classrooms now. Their wall is gone. The tanks
no longer roar down the streets whenever they please.

The streets are clean and in good repair. In every direction,
not too distant, is a border or the sea. The traveler

has been shown the maps, and every one shows
that the borders have never stayed the same for long.

The Traveler Encounters More Renowned Cities, Foreign Tongues, and Items of Historical Significance

"Ruins become the unconscious of a city, its memory, unknown, darkness, lost lands, and in this truly bring it to life."
—Rebecca Solnit, *A Field Guide to Getting Lost*
(all lines in italics are from this text)

1. *Without noticing it you have traversed a great distance . . .*

A thousand oaks to build the Vasa. Too many cannon, too little ballast, on her maiden voyage she swayed too much in a light breeze, took on water, capsized with thirty good souls. 1628.

A third of the millennium at the bottom of Stockholm harbor, miraculously unrotted in the brackish waters. Rediscovered, hauled up, restored and on display in a vast gray building.

The only surviving warship of her day. Fifteen euros and a ticket to Stockholm, you can see her too, looming in the dim space, dark from the preservatives, braced carefully, explained

in every detail, even the rescued bones visible under glass, faces reconstructed according to the best theories and techniques. *We believe their family members would recognize them,* say the signs.

2. *. . . the strange has become familiar . . .*

The handsome children of Tallinn walk the cobbles to school through the gray drizzle, not unhappily. They wave their cards

at the heavy door in the old wall, and it opens to let them in. They read about the forest brothers, camped miserable and hopeless

until the Russians ran them down, but their own brothers are in college or working the docks or the restaurants, sneaking a bottle

out of the house and down to the shore to meet their friends
and climb the crumbly concrete steps of the Linnahall, the mound

of concrete like a Mayan temple. The Russians threw it up
in 1980, for the Olympics that fizzled. They named it after Lenin

but that didn't last past '89. Thirty years and it's nearly rubble,
graffiti and broken glass, a sleazy night club and a great pile

of gray cement aimed like a broken spear at the gray Baltic.
The traveler clambers down the risky steps back toward

Old Town, where the ancient towers are rough but stubborn
and well tended. He hopes to be forgiven for thinking

of Ozymandias. What was that book, *The World as Will and Idea*?
An idea can make many shapes in the world. Two others

climb the stairs, stand in the wind, study the wide and bitter sea.

3. . . . *and the familiar if not strange at least awkward or uncomfortable,
an outgrown garment.*

Morning in Riga, M. sleeping, news of the home folks scanned, all well and good. Today they fly out to the north, another old and glorious and semi-famous city.

In the Garden Palace the creaky floors are the only drama. The traveler could sit on the gritty patio, commune with the crows and the steeples, which one can ascend from within for eight euros. But he's easy among the dark old walnut of the high room, at the inlaid desk he'd happily take home. A rough-hewn beam runs from floor to ceiling by the bathroom door.

Rooms like these, so quiet, the Nazis knocked and entered as they pleased, and the Russians too. Early morning, loud boots, stiff uniforms, we have your names, quickly now. A girl in nightgown and no shoes in the train car, another in three dresses and two coats. Some came back, lived to put on their best sweater and tell their story for a camera.

And the waiter is maybe 30, has lived in Azerbaijan, Turkey, London, Moscow. He likes the quiet here but the money is bad, who can live on 300 euros a month? The place was empty, Saturday lunch near the gleaming Art Nouveau embassies, a few people out with their kids or dogs. He brought dazzling servings of ice cream with fruit, three flavors, strawberries, oranges, kiwi, laid out like a dream on big white plates.

The Old Town is quiet at street level, but they found the right stairs down to a big cheap dinner, beer and wine among the young lovers and guys with ceramic pitchers of beer, the band setting up for later, red bricks rough with centuries of good noise.

They walked back into the misty night, half-lit streets, small knots of smokers and lovers, the overpriced amber and linen shops closed, the bars open and hopeful, the store selling black balsam and vodka lit up but empty, the girl behind the counter gazing into nothing, thinking of rivers or her boyfriend or God or suicide, how would he know.

Back at the Garden Palace the handsome blonde bellhop was still standing, too big for his clothes, too big for the spot where he waits all day for someone to need him, his boredom large as the city, neat as his one good suit, strong as his empty hands.

4. *The world is blue at its edges and in its depths. This blue is the light that got lost.*

Every door is blessed when no stranger comes through it to put you on a train against your will. Every threshold crossed by choice

is a gift of the god of trains, the god of doors, the god of early mornings
and stones. Every interior wall of rough stone is blessed,

every half-eaten sandwich left on the window ledge by somebody
long gone now. What's next is the question. Whose mother

and whose uncle are the questions. Whose language and whose tanks.
Whose money, whose boots and down coat, long for the dark months.

All of your questions will be answered, uncertainly and piecemeal.
On the day they came to Riga, bumping on the slow bus through

the birch thickets where the forest brothers hid, American tanks
rolled off a ship and onto the ancient streets. There is more to the story

but it hasn't happened yet. The traveler has tried to peer around
half-timbered corners, to catch a glimpse among narrow streets, towers,

cobbles that slow traffic and break heels, but all he finds is low sun,
blinding and almost warm, and a sky blue as desire, as history, as pain.

5. *He ceased to be lost not by returning . . .*

No man needs to hear his own language around him
every day of his life. In Tallinn they saw more old streets

and strollers the size of small cars, they learned of famous
Estonians with unfamiliar names. They found lunch at the Café

Josephine, fine French food since 1937, French ballads
instead of American pop, gilt rims on wine glasses

and grand bowls of pasta, cheese, and ham for eight euros.
A man should spend some time thinking that the talk

he cannot understand is brilliant discourse on the deepest
and most urgent topics, debates on the future of the euro,

confidences that will change lives forever, confessions
of true love, the craftiest seduction in centuries.

All this glimmers in golden fine syllables, shimmers
at the edges of his knowing, breaks like cold waves

on the dim city of his own words, its bland streets
and houses, churches with entry fees,

cheap hotels that still charge for breakfast,
bars full of silent drunkards.

6. . . . *but by turning into something else.*

And the traveler remembers belatedly
the city he has left out entirely,
a fine and lovely city full of people
who slide from their language to his
at his first awkward question,
who pull out their phones to show
the way to the tram or the ferry,
a place whose people have kept
the Russians from swallowing them
for centuries now, whose old fortress
island is now all beaches and museums,
easy strolls among the old battlements,
though to be sure the warriors
and weapons still inhabit other islands.
The Winter War is long over,
tanks rust in the northern lakes.
The Finns and their city glow
with good health and prosperity.

Fifty years now since anybody invaded.
Down the block is Sandro Kitchen,
its slogan *from the Baltics to Beirut*,
twenty euros for pizza man'ouche
with cilantro/ Zaatar/ Tabbouleh salad
w/ pomegranate/ Sesame hummus/
mint yoghurt/ zaalouk
or lamb ragout with organic egg/
goat cheese/ mint yoghurt/ pine nuts/
Tahini/ mint yoghurt/ pomegranate/
mint/ Saffron bread. M. and the traveler
smile across the table, struck again
by the pleasure of foods eaten
for the first time, by good wine
and food, *this is the life* they say
as they have said over and over,
knowing their great good fortune,
not knowing why it was given.

7. *All shall be blue round me, and in the midst of the blue world my heart . . . will beat gently.*

In 1535 sundogs appeared in the Stockholm sky, dazzling
and strange, captured by the painter Urban Målare.

The original is lost, but a good copy hangs in the city church,
two golden wheels in a sky restored now to a mottled blue

enigmatic as any great sign. The traveler woke to bright sun
on the ferry, dreamy islands passing out the window,

docks and houses layered with gold and chrome and
colors not to be named, spray on the window and his glasses

still by the bed, what world is this so vague and bright,
where is he, he should wake M. and show her but he looks

and looks and says nothing, thinks nothing, only sees
the blue of sky and the blue of sea and between them

the islands passing silent as ghosts, solid as thought,
grand and strange as will, as idea, as any heaven he can dream.

The Traveler Fails Kierkegaard Once and for All

To believe the self an entity ever becoming, never being,
dazzles me, as does the blaze of sun across the windows

of the distant building I thought was a church for weeks.
"We like living in the basement of awakening," wrote K.,

who thought despair the affect attached to doubt,
different from Angst, derived from Eng, narrowness,

Engel, Angel, Angina. If ignorance of despair is
the most common form of despair, and the true despair

is the desperation necessary to leap into the void
toward belief . . . then Kierkegaard, walking the cobbled

streets, a figure of renown and occasional suspicion.
Then the traveler, known to no one in this seaport town,

stalking toward the river and the muddy path along it,
smokestacks and factories producing obscure aromas

and indecipherable swirls of mist. There were always
fishermen, old and young, stoic in their gray boots,

quiet as tombs. Beaver-gnawed trees. Strollers,
and grandparents pushing them. Little knots of children

at the rocking horses, the swings, and the traveler
passing them all, hunched to his handlebars, bundled

for the cold, speaking to no one, quiet and quick on his way
and inexplicably, undeniably, faithlessly full of joy.

Abandoned Homeland

(2015)

The Body

> *and if we are not transformed, what is there to desire?*
> —John D. Caputo

Cool near the waterfall, creek louder than the highway.
Good in the dark, writing blind, everything close

and nothing clear. What else but to dream of another life
among such a roar, so much whelming water?

After dinner my friends talked of spiritual healing, of relief
from nagging pains and torments through a skillful touch,

manipulation of auras, so I told how my knee got sore
and swelled and clicked with every step for three days,

then slowly got better, all on its own. My story was
not well received, but I want to trust in mystery,

I wait each day for gifts I don't deserve, I am thankful
for lovely women who have healed me many times

without reiki or acupuncture or even looking my way.
I believe in auras near and distant, and that our souls

are bigger than our bodies. My wife called in the middle
of this, believe it or not, to say she'd fallen off the ladder

cleaning windows and broken her arm. She's home,
not in danger but entirely annoyed, with a temporary cast,

a sling, and a prescription for Vicodin. *Don't worry,*
she said. I believe and trust she will be made whole,

but I doubt anyone will cure her at a distance. *There are
miracles,* says Caputo, *and there are cheap parlor tricks.*

The water roars. I'm almost ready to walk to the rail,
my eyes are getting used to the dark, I am reckless sometimes

but not stupid. The body is more than some clay jar
with a dismal eternal glob inserted. It is to be trusted,

especially when it says *Not too fast*. The waterfall twists
and rumbles, alien, unstoppable, coming up stunned

and foaming on the rocks, broken into froth and magic
every second, hurrying onward as if not changed at all.

Contemplation with Old Honda, Carnality, Fish

Who can go free to the God behind God?
—Fanny Howe

1.
I have no excuse, just some coffee. Everybody is sleeping in.
I do not have a huge deal for a book about punctuation,

or the crappy ancient Civic we all think M. should dump
as soon as she gets the first check. She agrees. *But if I get*

*a real ca*r, she says, *I'll have to find a garage to park it in.*
I have no more penmanship than ideas about how to find

the God behind God, but almost always I can read the scratches
I leave behind, and the pages somehow fill up. The day is gray

but dry. A low branch tips, sways, settles. *The wind is what*
I believe in, said F. *"God" is the failure of all the other words.*

2.
Say Jesus had a wife. Would it mean one more reinforcement
of heteronormativity, another wearisome oppression to bear?

A divine affirmation of carnality and delight, the Holy One
and his mate sweating joyfully, sweetly together? I know

almost nothing of Jesus except that he spent little time
comforting the comfortable, or afflicting the afflicted.

3.
For the third time I pick up the cup and find it empty.
There are voices from the kitchen, bread, jam, more coffee,

I only need to stir myself. *I was lucky to be poor*, said L.,
and lucky to escape it. I was lucky too, I never had to live

on squirrels and dandelion leaves, though one whole winter
I had just three shirts. I remember opening the dresser

each school day, choosing one, thinking it was simple this way.

4.
The fish like it under water. The river doesn't spend
its days saying "I am beautiful." Who needs things?

English was not my first language, but I remember
only scraps of the others. There are voices that carry,

voices that carry meaning. No voice for my yearning
for some final grandeur. The trees nod without joy or sorrow,

absorb all the light they can. It changes. It will change.

Reading Neil Gaiman in a Western Suburb

"This is a bad land for gods," said Shadow.
—Neil Gaiman, *American Gods*

The condo is small, neat, uncluttered. The streets
are quiet at night--the cops keep the hoodlums

away from the school. Between the trees and clouds
we rarely see the mountains, and these days Mum talks

only about food and relatives, and Dad can be amazed
by a row of cars, a long hallway, cherries. So I like

to sit in the floral chair that came from Grandma
and Grandpa and to slip off into magic and drama,

sex and murder. I like to roam the continent,
Kansas to Wisconsin to the House on the Rock

and Lookout Mountain. I'm happy no stray god
wants me for a bodyguard or a nine-day vigil

strung up in the world-tree Yggdrasil. I'm glad
someone is up to the task, if only in a book I read

in mechanical, ghostly memory, patterns fleeting
and unsteady as the hero whose name is Shadow.

Both the story and the telling trouble my mind,
but in that old, odd way that even as a child

I yearned to be taken away, troubled and amazed.
The best country for gods is the country of the mind,

the story, a country where shapes move over streets
and cities, highways and mountains, empty lots

and chain stores, move like an ancient crow or red-tail,
keen, hungry, and entirely without words.

Thread

if my life is a thread being pulled by a needle . . .

If the chimes of freedom flash like the flash that caught you
half a mile from home last night, still circling the quarry,

wondering suddenly where the ducks and geese find shelter . . .
All you knew was to keep going, let the needle in your head

pull you onward, sweaty and puffing again, lucky, keeping
the pace you can, almost too fast, hoping to get lost in the music

or your worries and forget for a while the labor and sweat
and small pains, heel, knee, ankle, the swing of arm, thud,

thud on pavement, just keep on, follow the pull toward
the next turn, the next familiar street, forget the thunder

or wait for it after the flash, feel the breeze and know the storm
will find you if it chooses, wind in your face or not, let it go,

the rain is cool and the shirt is wet already with your hot sweat,
too late to slow down, too soon to think of home, cross

the steel bridge and take the little rise up Spring Street, pass
the small familiar homes like a silent crowd, like people sleeping

in the pews, left on Elm to the Catholic church, good people
filing in to sing and pray but you must go on, right on Lawn,

you know what pulls you now, you know this last long street,
the time is good, the legs are weary but they bear you on,

your heart is firm and strong, the air sweeps in and out
of your open, deep, and secret lungs and somehow still

your blood takes what it needs and gives the rest away.

Safety

I've lived my life in safe places, not at risk except for boredom and its associated disorders. The farm was safe, my room upstairs with my brother, the pale kitchen where we ate, maple cupboards my dad built and the plastic table we inherited and still fold our clothes on today. I have no tales of terror at home, no drunken parents, a bully or two but not such big deals really.

The dangers were from beyond, the ones that scared me: the Russians, the fallout from our own tests though we heard nothing about that until much later. God leaning down to decide whether I was worth saving.

Under the hot comforters my mother had stitched, below the leaky upstairs windows, I felt entirely safe from what I could see and exposed to everything I couldn't. The Russians were crazy, they didn't care if they died, they didn't want supermarkets or Jesus, all they wanted was to rule the planet whether it glowed like charcoal or not. And Jesus would never want anybody like me, willful and impolite to his teachers, sullen and recalcitrant in his secret heart, unable to resist saying the wrong thing too loud at the wrong time.

The stairs were gray painted wood, two of them broken a little and tilted enough that if you hit either one wrong in socks you'd slip and bang, bang, bang all the way down to the bottom and not much to console you there except Mom saying what, you fell down *again*?

Sniffle and suck it up, go back upstairs, through my sisters' room and into the spare room that was mostly empty except for my worldly uncle's trunk, which had nothing I was interested in but a heavy, hard, beautiful M-1 rifle pilfered from his time in Korea. It seemed absolutely perfect in its every curve of wood and steel, its mechanisms and rods and staffs, even its silence and refusal to do anything but shift in small ways and click gently, casually, confidently if cocked properly and its trigger pulled. It lacked only an agenda, a round, something to send off like a small, clear message to whomever it might concern.

What did I dream as I handled the weapon, lifted it to my shoulder, sighted down the barrel? I had fired guns, my own BB gun and the .22 my dad had for skunks. We were pacifists, the church taught, but nobody worried about plinking at cans and birds. These were the days when every third man was a veteran and the Good War was still fresh, and I had seen plenty of battles on TV. We played Swamp Fox and cowboys and Indians in the tall grass behind the house, arguing over who was dead and who wasn't.

Still, all I can bring back about the rifle is its feel in my hands, its weight and size and simple, ruthless, solid economy. Sooner or later it disappeared, but I don't remember that either, or much else about the world in those days beyond the open acres we farmed, the quiet fields and the noisy tractors, school and church and the books I lost myself in whenever I could. I don't even remember when I first discovered that even those distances were only the most partial, fragile, temporary shelter.

Ode with Winter Sunshine, One Mind, Four Houses

The winter birds, pleased by the sun.
Snow pushed off some of the sidewalks,

packed flat and slick on the rest,
minor ruts and chunks on the side streets.

The big red house, the little white house,
the yellow brick house and the red brick house

all seem delighted to have made it this far,
mainly intact, furnaces roaring quietly

in their cellars, shingles locked
in place, doors mostly latched.

The houses might be saying
We have ridden out another night,

and that seems strange and hopeful
when once again the streets are

passable if not clear, the walks
are passable if not clear, and a little man

in a long blue coat wanders by,
a little late as always, snug in his jeans

and boots and sweater, his mind
passable, passable if not clear.

Contemplation with Acorns and Guitar

Night gathers in the pines, but the grassy slopes aren't ready
to give up. The fireflies and the frogs have things to do.

I have a good post to lean on, a stolen pen, lots of paper.
Tomorrow we'll explain, apologize, surrender. Tomorrow

the heat will return, and fat men will tell expensive lies to make
themselves richer. Tomorrow more cattails will die,

more glaciers will calve, acorns will fall from the trees.
The rhythm of the world has nothing to do with saints,

everything to do with bodies. Even on a single path
there are always more than two ways. One law is waiting.

One law is doing something, right now. Maybe it's opening
your eyes, after all these years. Maybe standing up, or sitting

in the packed privacy of the trees, in the places between,
places where things breathe on their way to the sky.

When we start back the air fills with something not fog,
not dust, filmy, almost light, all real, the secret net

of the world shaken out just for us. Let it all stay soft,
let it linger and shimmer around us. Let it all stay.

The page almost glows in the last light, it crazes and
glitters, reads itself without me, it soaks in my words

and gives back something else. Even the birds know better
than to speak this late. It's not dark. It's only less brilliant

than it was. Remember that kid you called dumb? We are
all asleep in the outward man. We are all deaf in the world

of light. Even in the darkness it's hard to hear what
we need. There are words to love: *willow, bullfrog,*

mud. Things that lie waiting for centuries, like a fiddle
forgotten in an attic, barely breathing in the heat,

the dark. It isn't lost. What's a century or two?
Not every tree has a guitar inside. But some of them do.

Cookies

   —after Neruda

I'm tired of being respectable. And professional.
For too long I've gone into classrooms and bathrooms
and churches, smiling and brittle as a garden gnome,
or a homecoming queen waving to the cold bystanders.

The aura of solid houses makes my insides quiver.
I want to walk into every one--houses I've passed by
for twenty years and never entered.
I want to sit in the big recliners, steal cookies
from the jars on kitchen counters, riffle through magazines,
check in medicine cabinets and under beds
for scandalous revelations.

I'm tired of being available. And polite.
I'm ready to be invisible, grouchy, and stupid.
I'm ready to stand up in the middle of the meeting
and scratch myself on the way out the door.
I'm ready to bring my guitar to class, set up between
the students and the door, play every song
I've ever played, every song I can remember,
without explanation or apology, whether or not
I remember the chords or can hit the high notes.
"Louie, Louie." "Kumbaya." All nine verses
of "Stuck inside of Mobile with the Memphis Blues Again."

I'm ready to be a bad wizard, to change morons
into moonshine, dutiful drudges into parsley,
solid citizens into Corvettes and cottonmouths.
I'm ready to fill up with gas on the way out of town
and stick to the township roads, so narrow
that somebody has to take the shoulder.
To drive a wide spiral until I find God

or Lake Erie or the providential,
proverbial, preverbal Mississippi,
so low now I can barrel right across it
with barely a splash or a slither and sail on
into the blue-gold American night.

Letter from an Ohio Classroom

Such an attitude stems from a tragic misconception of time,
from the strangely rational notion that there is something in the
very flow of time that will inevitably cure all ills.
—Martin Luther King, Jr.

I'll let you be in my dream if I can be in your dream.
—Bob Dylan

The theme for the day is not dream but time, time in its magisterial
indifference, sacred or profane only as we make it, shape it,

as we read its scars, its tracks, its dreamy traces. *How is it
with the nothing?* Heidegger asked. *Where shall we seek*

the nothing? We may not comprehend the ensemble of beings,
he said, *but we find ourselves in the midst of beings all the same.*

He wasn't in my dream as we talked about injustice anywhere,
direct action, creative tension. I imagined shutting down

the government out of fear that poor people would get health care
and so destroy the country. I said nothing about that.

One guy complained that he couldn't bring his deer rifle
on campus. *Prejudiced against rednecks,* I heard him mutter,

and found myself suggesting that he just keep it in his trunk.
A guy in the first row shook his head. Somebody read the part

about getting all the facts before taking action. When I asked
for an example and the guy in the first row said "Girls,"

a stir ran around the room, but then we shrugged and smiled.
We'd all been there, we admitted, blacks and whites, guys

and dolls. Some of us lived in the midst of beings we could
not comprehend. One of us hated her stepfather even more

than her brother did, but kept up a mask of mere hostility,
seething, sullen, lest she be thought lacking in respect.

We all knew time would not cure our ills. We all wanted
to be in somebody's dream. We all had trunks full of guns

and time and being, full of nothing, nothing to hide.

Fifty Billion Planets

The galaxy is crawling with life. What's for dinner?
                                        —Anonymous

Hemingway was wrong about the very rich, and when he walked
into my nonfiction class I told him so. He wanted to punch me,

but I told him all physical violence on campus was prohibited
by the Peaceful Menno Code, so he just glared and stomped

out the door. The Code also prohibits gloating, so I asked
the students what we'd learned. "You blew our chance to talk

to a famous dead guy," said the smart kid. "And a rich one," said
Melinda, who never said anything. "Yeah, but rich people *aren't*

like you and me," I answered, weakly. "You mean they don't
attach lame adverbs to their speech tags?" said the smart kid.

I opened my mouth to tell him off graciously, within the guidelines
of the P. M. C., but just then the door opened and a sweet voice

said, "Qu'ils mangent de la brioche." I was baffled, but the Code
requires unconditional intercultural affirmation, so I smiled

and nodded. The woman sashayed towards me, glittering
as she walked. Fifty billion earthlike planets in the galaxy

and there she was, a golden, liquid comet on a collision course
with my poor sinful earth. She circled me, twice, and then she

was more like a hawk pondering whether it was worth the effort
to swoop down and snatch a meadow vole. The students

were spellbound, Hemingway forgotten. "Everyone thinks
you said, 'Let them eat cake,'" I muttered. "Everyone in your

stupid country, maybe," she answered. "As if the whole world speaks your silly language." She slid a finger from my ear

to my chin, and I shivered, but then she turned to the class, and she was not at all a vain, dead queen. "There are

fifty billion earthlike planets in the Milky Way," she said. "How will you spend your small, strange, unrepeatable life?"

Abandoned Homeland of Exiles

How else to describe this absurd, lovely world? And yet
the trees stir themselves into the humid air, take the weather

as it comes. Maybe it'll kill them, but not today. Praise
for the mutilated planet is insufficient but essential.

I'm all in favor of grief, mercy, and language, but what kind
of meal do they make? Whose children will they save

from minimum wage or the poverty draft? Still, it's the season
when despite all my moans and whines the rooms fill up

with strange and lovely faces and we revel in the happy
weariness of learning names, explaining badly, bearing

our loads of ill-defined matter and impractical passions
like sticks and tinder for the illegal fire we hope to burn

when we find that lost hollow, the clearing with three rows
of skinned logs for seating, fire ring, blackened kettle.

Yes, the trail's overgrown, root-rough, yes there might
be snakes, yes mosquitos for sure. Wear jeans and socks.

Bring the guitars, the song sheets. Uncle Jim will say
something genial, solid, and a little awkward. We'll sing

and sway, praise each other and walk back in the dark,
holding hands. Then we'll gather what we need and head

off again, for good. The exit doors will open if we push
and wait and push again. Let the alarm bells blaze.

They'll stop us. But they'll have to let us go.

Three for Trakl

1.
Like the burrowing of a field mouse or a mole,
the woman searching her gray bag for the slippers

she left beside the bed. Like searching Trakl
for a line without desolation and beauty:

rotten branches, holy brother, gentle lyre-play.
Now the left-handed women are quiet,

writing carefully in their small notebooks,
recording the three important dreams they dreamt

while rain spattered and trembled in the downspouts.
Madness, lonely, dying. Ruin, darkness, stars.

2.
Against all logic, Trakl is unusually translatable.
He was crazed in that peculiar modern way:

aware that disaster was bearing down, escape
was impossible, beauty and God as useless

as trenches and machine guns. Red wine,
ether, veronal: precious and insufficient.

Her face is floating through the waters.
Her hair is waving in bare branches.

What garden, what sister, what mountain
could deflect or distract him? *Like a wound*

her mouth is open. His life a limping journey
toward one doorway, a vast room heaped

with the stinks and groans of empire burst and blown
through the flesh of farmers and schoolboys.

Heal us, they surely begged, help us. He had
some rags, his hands, water. He knew the doses

and protocols for opium, ether, he could see
the neat rows of bottles on shelves in Vienna,

far away, so clear. He had nothing, some odd lines
from his own poems, fragments of Grete's piano

echoing in the lost upstairs rooms in Salzburg.

3.
Almost impossible to sit still. Chilly rain, October,
the furnace balky in this borrowed house. We huddle

at the stove, put on our jackets, make futile phone calls.
All over Salzburg bronze plaques on walls hold

Trakl's poems up to the rain, the sunshine,
the Föhn wind that still kicks up in autumn,

bearing dust and melancholy. We are in no danger,
but we talk of failed systems, bitter nights

and blunders, leaks and disasters. The empire
creaks and groans, pumps straining at nothing,

brown bitter fluids spilling from the pipes.

[Passages in italics are from *The Poems of Georg Trakl,* tr. Margitt Lehbert, 2007.]

Ambitions

These are woods that forgive everything but forget nothing.
  —Tomas Tranströmer

To be a forest dense and green enough to hide a million creatures

To be the vine grown right to the top of the tallest tree

To be the man whose job is to save the tree by sawing through the vine three feet up

To be the bench waiting just when a man needs a rest

To be the sign that answers the question the man hasn't asked yet

To carry back the names: willow, buttonbush, boxelder maple, spatterdock and fragrant waterlily

Water smartweed and the endangered wapato, midge and mayfly and whirligig beetle

Green darner dragonfly, vivid dancer damselfly

And always the large dim roar of many narrow waves hurrying in

To stand at the edge until one laps at my shoes

To touch the water and think *I could swim*

To cross back over the barrier beach, the only human sound my footsteps

Many insects, a high gentle wind stirring everything

Countless volunteers, the last sign remembers

To volunteer at last

The Mysteries in Yellow Springs

> *"Rat!" he found breath to whisper, shaking. "Are you afraid?"*
> *"Afraid?" murmured the Rat, his eyes shining with unutterable*
> *love. "Afraid! Of Him? O, never, never! And yet—and yet—O,*
> *Mole, I am afraid!"*
> —Kenneth Grahame, "The Piper at the Gates of Dawn,"
> *The Wind in the Willows*

The buskers on Xenia Ave. had a new song:
At least it's not as hot as yesterday! It was still hot

but the spring was still cold, the girl dumped her water bottle
to fill it with the iron-dense water. *I don't like it*

but I want it, she explained to grandma. Baby sister
reached toward the shiny stream, looked back at Mom

to be sure it was OK. The water kept saying something
small but insistent to the rocks. Susan told me that the rocks

were all set in place not long ago, that there's a buried
tank, that the handy strand everybody drinks from

was designed that way. Well, that's helpful, I wanted
to tell her. It's hard to tell if the rocks agree or are grateful

for the company or are bored to tears. They are orange
from the iron, not blushing or confused. Like the girl

with half her head shaved, they don't care who looks.
They might be the shelving steps nearby, the ones

nobody notices and everybody walks on. They might be
buried anywhere, with worms and moles for company.

They might be here when the Piper steps out at last,
goat-footed and dappled, shining like sun through

new leaves, too strange and grand to look in the face.

Meditation on Narrative, Dogma, and Flight

It is still beautiful to hear the heart beat
but often the shadow seems more real than the body.
     —Tomas Tranströmer

My people are not natural storytellers.

Ask my father for a story, he's still trying to get it going
when all the boys have drifted off to the kitchen.

Still, I want the reader as far inside of my skin as possible,
no matter the difficulties. For instance:

The self does not feel like matter, but that's all it is.
I forget who said so, and I don't agree,

but it was spoken with such confidence.

And so much else needs to be considered:

Kites make the wind visible.
Some tree frogs can only sing for three nights.

Can you tell me how it is that light comes into the soul?

(That was Thoreau, 1851.)

Spirit is to religion as love is to marriage.

How do you run faster? Start running faster.

How does the box kite manage to fly?

"This is wonderful" and "this must continue" are close kin.

And then the kite's shadow across the plowed earth.

Brief History of Midwestern Civilization

Grandpa's Ford panel truck was powder blue
and held exactly six chicken coops, the wooden

kind that would hold fifteen or twenty
near-grown pullets, or the cardboard boxes

full of yellow chicks. We could get many more
in our red F-150, but if it rained they got wet.

Grandpa knew everything about chickens
and a whole lot about everything else, how

to buy ice cream, how to let me adjust
the heat in his car, also a Ford. He knew

how to do everything but keep his heart
beating. And so he was gone. And so

because or in spite of all this the fields
behind our house sprawled out for miles,

peaceful as cows even when we got rid
of the cows, the fields bare and gray

in winter, the snow scoured off by wind,
the fences yanked up, the fence rows

piled and burned. Then spring, the corn
implanted and the black fields flushed

with ammonia, lush in August
as a jungle that only knows one word.

Further Notes on the Martyrs

Our speaker has a tongue screw with him, though
it is a replica. He speaks of spectacle, witness,

dying well. One group's criminals . . . Stories
are not preserved by accident. Heroes are made

necessary by the nature of memory. Life is stronger
than death, and that is why we must praise.

I think. Identity depends on memory,
which depends. You might get in the book

if you merely suffered. We strive to maintain
an empathetic view of the oppressors, but we believe

that truth is real and can be known and practiced.
Therefore we praise the martyrs and the beauty

of holiness, even the beauty of rose windows
and artful representations of the Cross.

When the grieving villagers sing Holy, Holy, Holy
over the mass grave, surely this is beautiful,

though we cannot clearly say why. We cannot
believe that death is the mother of beauty,

the lovely wound that sends the child in search
of poetry. Surely we shall know the truth,

if not now in the place of fire, on the pages
of fire, in the voices and bodies on fire, in the ashes

where the child bends for the tongue screw,
in the moment when he grasps the iron,

still warm, and straightens to show his brother.

Something Is

The wood smoke smells so good it's like a meal.
The beach open and empty, a few gulls bobbing,

one fisherman. Wavelets ripple in with their small news:
the world still awash with inscrutable information.

Half-heard voices from under the rainfly, three young men
at ease between breakfast and lunch, clink of the campstove,

Yeah, good idea. Ow, Lord! Scuffed tracks in the sand.
Horsefly shares the bench with me, just a moment.

A. said she wrote about goddesses for years, and never
even noticed. *Really,* she says, *I recognized myself*

just last Saturday for the first time. The alphabet
took us into the rigid plain of our left brains,

like a thousand-acre cornfield, and we've been
stuck in the flats among the monochromes and

right angles, people of the line and the book.
The world has only one page. It is not best read

left to right, top to bottom. It has many seams and edges,
places where secrets and treasures may be found if one

walks slowly, alone or with a lover or your dogs
whose names are Norman and Under. *We all make*

something out of nothing, said G.C., a true believer.
Unlike him I'm full of earnest doubt, and sure I can

make nothing except out of something, especially
when I cannot say just what that something is.

Waterfall

So I didn't get the instructions. So the pond's full
of grainy duckweed, bumblebees in damp clover,

dragonflies and damselflies, twittery birds. Young Will
keeps saying things like "This could be lava!" Two hawks

swoop and soar. I think they might see paradise
just over the brow of the hill, and because I'm not

Kafka if I could climb those skies myself the mighty
keeper at the gate would usher me in graciously, show me

to the holy sun porch where God and I would sit, drink
coffee and compare our griefs, our big defeats and

little victories. And the sweet air will zephyr all round us,
carrying birdsong and creek babble, and we will agree

that things are dismal but not unusual, and that a certain
cockeyed hope is still required of us. We'll walk a long way

through the beeches and tulip poplars, and at the waterfall
we will peel our clothes and splash in the shallows,

as close as we dare to the roar and rush, and its every
syllable will come clear suddenly. And then everyone

will be there, your friends and mine, our enemies too,
all the strangers holy and unholy, and in the water's spell

we will touch our perfect bodies and our minds and
remember everything. And we will laugh and dance

and make meta- and physical love until the very universe
shivers and glows. And when at last we are healed, sated,

complete, we will lie down in the long meadow grass,
the dragonflies basking and soaring all round, and sleep

in the roar and the silence for as long as our dreams require.

Without a Plea

(2019)

Plain Advice

Don't be foolish. No, be foolish.
Each of these trees was once a seed.

Look down the road till it's all mist and fumes:
of course your journey is impossible.

It's stupidly hot for September and yet here's
an eddy, a gust, something to stir you

as the high leaves of the walnut are stirred,
as fine droplets touch you, touch the table

and the deck, no explanation, no design.
And beauty is like God, mystery

in plain sight, silent, hesitating
in leaves and the shadows of leaves,

in the carved fish painted and nailed
to the railing, in skeins of cloud

and searching fly and pale blue
scrim of sky and seas of emptiness

and dazzle, fusion and spin,
fire and oblivion and all that lies

on the other side of oblivion.

Late Summer with Mink, Duende, and Calamities of Varying Degree

> *Seeking the duende, there is neither map nor discipline. We only know it burns the blood like powdered glass . . .*
> —Federico Garcia Lorca, "Theory and Play of the *Duende*"

Sometimes there's a dead cicada on the driveway
near the back door, iridescent, almost weightless,
and that's only the beginning.

If you want the *duende*, sometimes you have to stamp your feet.
Sometimes you just have to look around, wildly or not.

Someday you'll look at the bulk pack of batteries and then just buy two,
so your children won't have to deal with the leftovers.

I think mink must be lonesome, sometimes, and hungry most of the time.

Don't fight when you're hungry. Don't drink when you're angry.
Don't dig into the chips until your wife goes to bed.

To speak of trees is almost a crime, said Brecht, *when there is so much injustice.*
He was right, but *almost* is the important word.

Sometimes the wild, silky part of yourself can't resist
sneaking into the henhouse and killing all the pullets.

The editor said Marianne Moore lied, that she didn't hate poetry,
but what did he know?

It's not the worst thing to admit that you hate what you love most.

The word *sometimes* belongs somewhere in that sentence.

My friend Ray says he needs finer wire mesh around his henhouse.
The mink was slender enough to sneak in.
The pullets were six weeks old, too big to drag out.

The mink killed seventy, one after another,
but couldn't take a single one off to feast on.

The hogs ate well that week.

"Nothing Is Level There"
–Bob Dylan, on Duluth

Consider the world as an evil tree. Hans Denck did, in 1560.
"It has never borne as much evil fruit as in our day,"

he wrote. "But there is not that much to bewail us yet.
There is more, by far, to be thankful for." The gray skies

of Duluth, yes, and the mysterious foghorns, and the slanting
streets. Or the joys of living far from the big lake and its

merciless howl, in the flat corner of a state that is nowhere
so crooked, where the creeks can barely decide which way

to run, where the swells and dips of the mother's soft body
are enormous and arcane as the sky, where winter trees

twist into the pale clouds. So it is necessary to be grateful.
And to see the world clearly. And to dream of the great change

but avoid the error of the Israelites, the golden calf that
Moses burned and ground to powder and forced them

to drink. What *am* I drinking, I wonder some days, when
the coffee has an edge that seems new and unsavory,

uncanny even. Will this carry me off, end my years of ease
and comfort, cast me into the long spiral? Not so far from here

the Russians are bombing hospitals. Not so long ago
we bombed a hospital. The explanations were plentiful

but not convincing. *The world is an evil tree* works as well
as any. "Truthfulness is crucial," wrote C. D. Wright,

recently deceased, in a book I read closely but had almost forgotten. "The tree has never borne so much evil fruit,"

said Hans Denck in 1560. And still there is not that much to bewail us. Still we shall be thankful for the crooked streets,

for the broad waters, for the deep and irregular earth.

Mud and Gravel

1.
Gravel and mud, mud mixed with gravel, gravel sinking gray and jagged into the soft brown mud as the spring storms beat down and pass by, as puddles fill and ebb away, as the heavy yellow diggers and draggers and loaders prowl in their loud slow way. This sloppy wide mess that runs down one side of the creek, across the sidewalk and the street and back the other side of the creek will be for the good of all--so we are told and mainly believe. The storm waters and the foul waters should not mingle.

The mess is temporary, we believe, the costs manageable. The mud and gravel and slimy tracks and branches broken, trees uprooted and undermined, all these are small and temporary against the greater good, against keeping our sour and difficult wastes sealed off from the innocent rain.

So we pick our way, try to ease our minds. This is not the Somme after all. Any day now the green pipes and the concrete junctions will be laid and joined and covered, the mud leveled and smoothed. The new grass will be sowed and sprouted, the sidewalks patched, saplings planted where the lost trees stood.

We have seen the old photos, the bare fields that are wooded now, the fresh streets, the first rough buildings. We close our eyes and can almost remember those days and the days before, the days of no streets and no village, only the deep woods and wetlands, traces the deer follow to the water, to the clearings where they browse at dusk and dawn, their faces lifting solemnly at what might have been the whisper of a stealthy paw, of a moccasin.

2.
A hundred years ago my country entered the Great War. This morning the radio told of horses and mules shipped over the ocean

to drag machines and food and men through the mud, the splatter, the broken bits of trees and men, flowers and guns.

In 1914 the entire British Army owned 80 motor vehicles. Between 1914 and 1917 the U. S. shipped 1000 horses a day to Europe, many of them half-tamed animals from the Great Plains.

The horses were so valuable that the Germans plotted to infiltrate the docks at Newport News, to infect the horses with anthrax and glanders.

The plot failed, but 8 million horses died in the war, plus countless mules and donkeys—better suited for conditions on the front, but like the horses, large and attractive targets. Very few were volunteers.

3.
No man or animal was suited for the mud of Flanders, the mud of Passchendaele, the mud that was a slime of dirt and shit and piss and blood, iron and casings and shrapnel and flesh in all stages of disintegration.

The mud was *sucking* wrote Siegfried Sassoon, wrote Herbert Read, wrote Richard Aldington, wrote Wilfred Owen. It entered through the mouth, the eyes, the skin. Men sank in to their knees, and deeper. Men foundered and despaired. One was trapped for 65 hours before being rescued.

Hell is not fire, hell is mud, wrote someone in a trench newspaper.

Tolkien, at the Somme with the Fusiliers, caught trench fever and was sent home. Much later he had Sam Gamgee come face to face with dead things, dead faces, in the stinking mire of the Dead Marshes.

4.
My room is quiet this morning. The machines are still as stones, the wind tugs at the Douglas fir and the bald cypress near my window. The mud runs along the creek, this side and the other, like the scars of surgery on the largest animal anywhere.

To get here I walked around the yellow tape, the orange pylons, over the raked gravel waiting between the wooden forms.

I have seen, we have seen, the earth heal and change. Flanders is lovely again. Things grow from the mud. New greens erupt irresistible as gravity, as rain, as love.

Every mess is not a crisis. Eggs must be broken. Today is not tomorrow, or yesterday. Everything is connected, and every thing is precisely itself.

5.
Like the mud and the gravel, the creek and the trees, like you and everyone you love and despise, I am spinning through space and time on a course too fast and wild for any sober reckoning.

I have a good bed, and no rifle. The wars are a long way from here. My shoes are only a little muddy.

Further Inquiries into Duende

Never pretend to be a unicorn by sticking a plunger on your head.
—Martín Espada

It is not a question of aptitude, but of style. . . . Tired of lies and circles, Descartes fled along the canals to listen to the singing of drunken sailors.
—Federico Garcia Lorca

In Juneau we walked the boardwalk along the surging stream,
both banks lined with prettified former whore houses.

A bald eagle perched on a post, severe and indifferent.

I wouldn't dare tell the scruffiest bald eagle it lacked *duende*.

My students have many opinions about *duende*,
though we failed to come up with a concise definition.

Does *Phantom of the Opera* have *duende*? R: Yes. C.: No.

Can you achieve *duende* through feedback and distortion? Me: No.
    R.: Maybe.

Bach more than Brahms. But not all Bach, either.

Marley's "I Shot the Sheriff." Clapton's, well . . . But "Layla," both
    electric and acoustic.

Beyonce, but not Britney.

Prince, that solo on "While My Guitar Gently Weeps."

Keats *and* Yeats. And Blake, almost too much.

Walt and Emily, both. Dark chocolate vs. a huge potluck with lots of desserts and baked beans and potato salad that maybe has been sitting out too long.

The Stones and the Beatles. But really, John more than Mick.

Soybeans, no. Wheat, no. Corn, in a bumper year.

The Rockies, sure. The Smokies, here and there.

In the prairies, only the sky.

The Listener at the Conference on Peacebuilding, or Playing the Spider

Till the bridge you will need be form'd, till the ductile anchor hold,
Till the gossamer thread you fling catch somewhere, O my soul.
—Walt Whitman, "A Noiseless Patient Spider"

1.
According to the people from Dakar, Bogata, Kolkata, etc., my town in the Ohio fields may not be the center of the world.

One asks, *I traveled for forty-one hours to speak for fifteen minutes?* So we listen hard for fifteen minutes.

Flinging threads into the void seems so 19th century. And yet, to catch hold somewhere . . .

2.
Would you rather be a button, a hook, or an eye?

In the end, the eye sees too much. The ear cannot close. The body cannot refuse to be touched.

When the bad daughter escapes, what does she do with the rest of her life?

Someone said: *it is easier to love the deprived in far corners of earth than our own inconvenient children.*

Your failure may open a window to the soul.

If we can tell the stories simply, without explanation . . .

The man who survived the concentration camp watched *Hogan's Heroes* with his granddaughter, years later, both of them laughing.

A groundhog dwells under the rocky ledge just outside the apartment door.

3.
The oppressive community is itself complicated, but the shunned find this small comfort.

Wind moves. Sand whispers.

Sometimes there may be no clear, efficacious, nonviolent solution.

I will only ask God to forgive them, said Miriam.

Who will be the conscientious objectors in the wars against women, against the poor, against the planet?

4.
Sometimes the silence of mourning is all we can offer.

Can we eroticize peace?

Everything is connected, but not even the wind harp can say exactly how.

To build soil from dust and ashes.

To argue with God and the world as it is.

To notice the groundhog, and let it be.

God Is Not Right, He Is Big

The news isn't all bad. July and August
were the hottest months in human history,

but a family found the pet tortoise
that went missing in 1982. The low cloud

above me passes under the high clouds
like a souped-up Civic passing on the right.

I've been all over this island and still
have no names for most of the trees.

Despite the urgings of good people
I do not find Job comforting: all that

swag and bluster, mean and useless
as Oz before Toto pulls the curtain.

The plenitude and manifold texture
of things, this comforts me a little.

My old friend is in a hospice bed,
his beard gray and wispy.

His blond granddaughters, both born
months early, are up too soon,

happily demanding love and cereal.
The low cloud is nearly past,

the high clouds are scattered and lit
by the early sun. Not everyone is safe.

Not everyone is warm. "God is not big,
he is right," that wise fool William Stafford

had the dandelions say, but they were
already drying up, forgetting

everything, loosing their frothy seeds
to scatter and settle as they might.

Elegy in Two Places and Two Parts

And sometimes, even music cannot substitute for tears.
-Paul Simon

1. Quarry Hollow, Kelleys Island

Word is, the owners were only here twice this summer.
I had to pull the door out from behind the bed and

lean it up in the frame. At least they ripped out the old,
disgusting carpet, and the new floor's still pretty clean.

For once we made the 6:00 ferry, though I forgot
the fresh mozzarella I was supposed to sprinkle

on the casserole. Gregg is still in the hospice bed,
his uneven breathing all that's left. Today a student

read her poem about her artist roommate's crafty pen
and I remembered Gregg turning clay on the wheel,

talking as his hands centered and shaped it, graceful
and efficient as a hawk carving circles in the air.

It's muggy, the window ledge is full of mold, the foldout
bed is mushy and dingy, the wine glasses are plastic.

There was a dead mouse in the upstairs toilet.
And I'm feeling like the guy who fell from the silo

and lived, like the Christmas spruce nobody picked
before it got too big for anyone's living room.

2. Maple Grove Cemetery

We parked in the wet grass, found the little urn
his father made. It was propped on a box

next to Gregg's parents' stone, out in a far corner.
A scrim of trees, the browning fields beyond.

The family was late, as they always are—
We were just talking and forgot the time, Karen said.

There were a few white chairs, some scripture,
some words from the interim pastor, a decent guy

with a trim beard who barely knows any of us.
It's not his fault. I read the poem I'd brought,

and we sang two verses of "Amazing Grace."
After the prayer someone nodded and pointed

through the trees, and when I shifted I saw
what I hadn't seen, two full-sized white-tails

and two half grown, all of them watching us
with that enigmatic earnest look deer have.

Do quiet beings always seem wise to noisy ones?
We considered each other for a little while.

Then Karen and the children got up, bent one by one
to touch the urn, and we followed them away.

And I thought: the deer knew we would be here,
they came in hope that we might join them,

step through the thin line of trees,
cross the field into that other life.

The God of Dirt

came up to me & scowled
and asked me what we'd done
with the treasure. Sorry,
I said, I can't even
tell you where it went,
Lake Erie, the St. Lawrence,
we barely noticed.

Well then, said the god
of dirt, *taste & see*
& there she was,
unknown & yet
I knew her,
had seen her
in some hollow of the mind,
flitting & calling,
& not for me,
not to me.

Listen said the god
of dirt & she sang
liquid & lovely
tangled up my body
& mind in blue
and gold and green
thickets of song.

Then she whispered
something soft to me
& spun herself away,
whispered to me
something soft
that I will not say.

Where I Was Instead

> *Late have I loved you, beauty . . . You were in fact inside me,*
> *but I was not inside you.*
> —St. Augustine, *The Confessions*

I was forgetting to register, forgetting to order books,
forgetting to turn off the lights on my way to bed.

I was still somewhere on the Pennsylvania Turnpike,
stuck among four semis in a snow squall, barreling

down a mountain curve at 77 miles an hour, the little car
skittering with each gust. I was waking up every hour

to blow my nose and pee, navigating interior caverns
dripping with yellow snot. I was eating too many chips,

checking scores on my phone, flicking through photos
of people I didn't know. I was reading the laments

of young mothers worn down by the second baby, the job,
the house, the first kid still in diapers. I was avoiding

the real, bitter news, the trickling glaciers, the manifold
miseries, the grinning orange nemesis, just for today.

I was listening to Caleb my firstborn grandson explain
how he drove the giant tractor right out on the road,

how he saw the Arch so big you can see it from everywhere.
I was watching Owen laugh and pick up berries with

the salad tongs, eat them one by one, sing as he forked
in pieces of pancake, come thou fount of every blessing,

banging the table, laughing, tune my heart, he's not yet two
and yet he has the tune down flat, also some of the words

and all necessary expression, I laughed and sang and beat
time with him, oh, come thou fount, oh tune my heart.

Late Spring in Old River Town with Guesswork and Bombay Sapphire Gin

The poet reads a poem called "Snow," full of metaphor
and light. Behind him is a big old window and behind that

a tree, its leaves twisted just out of shape by the uneven
old float glass. Not metaphor but things, I guess, not things

but the way things are seen and pressed into language
like keys into wax. The poet's arms are behind his back.

Maybe God woke up, he says. I may be remembering wrong,
confusing distance with death. The stars are a night

full of guesses. The leaves do exactly what they do,
and so does the window. Only to the watcher is it strange.

Only in Madison, Indiana, a river town that used to be
something. There was the broad Ohio, the Michigan road,

the riverboats and the factories and then the railroad,
before the other railroad came, and then all the other roads

that passed it by. People still find mussel shells with round holes
where buttons were drilled from them. Now the riverboat

restaurant won't open till two on Saturday. *Too much rain
this morning*, said the waitress, *the cook is still working on the fryers.*

We can come back, but won't. In the Filling Station
liquor store the clerk said she loves the Bombay Sapphire

I brought to the counter, but can't afford to drink it.
I knew that for three drinks in the hotel bar I could get

the whole bottle, so I just smiled, and she smiled back,
and I walked back to our room on the second floor

of the Riverboat Inn. My wife and I poured our glasses full,
then went to sit on the balcony, the two of us alone

with the quiet night, the distant river. And the darkness
eased into town, and then, as if God had awakened, the storm.

Determinism on a Summer Morning in the Midwest

1.
There's no such thing as free will and that's bad, or so says
Stephen Cave in *The Atlantic*. I guess that explains my decision

to read his whole grim article this morning, when I had plans
to walk around town, mail a package, buy a retirement card

for Susan, have a cup of coffee uptown as I always think
I should but rarely do. The problem, says Cave, isn't that

we don't *have* free will but that we need to think we do.
"It seems that when people stop believing they are free agents,

they stop seeing themselves as blameworthy for their actions."

2.
Dostoyevsky said, *If God is dead, everything is permitted,*
but the claim has not been proven to my satisfaction.

There are tulips and a daffodil on the table, in a glass
mostly full of water. There's a child's orange coat hanging

by the door. Who can say when the gates will open,
or what they'll reveal? Lisa's five or six tables away,

but her voice is the only one I can hear. Not the words,
just the tone. She passed along what sounds like bad news,

though not a catastrophe. What am I doing here?
Anywhere? It feels like I'm free, but only because

I have no idea what to do next. OK, I have several
ideas, just none that seem halfway interesting.

Out on the sidewalk a woman with a child's hand
clutched in hers passed one way, then back the other.

3.
Blonde on Blonde is fifty years old. Dylan is still touring.
There are songs that mean more to me than most

of the Bible. I have fair-sized chunks of the Bible
and dozens of Dylan songs "by heart," which means

"lodged in my brain, to emerge at unpredictable moments."
Should I leave them by your gate? Should I wait?

4.
I have to go pee or just go home. There's nobody at home,
nobody in my office, I'd be safe either place, it would

seem like I could do anything I wanted. Maybe not
disappear, or fly, or grow hair on the top of my head.

I could get in the car and drive straight north to the lake,
or cross the bridge to Canada, or take the small roads

across the open prairies till they dwindle into traces.

5.
MS Word fixes some of my typos, but not all of them.
People I know keep wandering along the sidewalk.

The woman I thought was Susie isn't. The sky
is gray but no rain yet. The spring has been miserable.

I pay young folks to mow, spread mulch, things I could do
but just don't want to. I get on the bike and tear around

the country roads instead, come home sweaty and pleased
with myself. The tomatoes are still in their little plastic pots.

The broccoli is leggy and sulking. Who wants to believe
it's all my fault? Who wants to believe it isn't?

6.
"Wherever you go, you take yourself with you,"
says Neil Gaiman, also "You can't make me love you."

I'm pretty sure that when he said you he didn't mean me.

7.
For years I've loved the notion of being lost,
thanks to Rebecca Solnit's *Field Guide to Getting Lost,*

not to mention Jesus and Thoreau. I've lived for decades
in the same house on the same street in the same town

but I've never quite gotten my head around being saved.
In an old poem I wrote something like "He decided to save

his soul, the way some people save / handkerchief boxes . . ."

8.
"Sleep," says Picard-as-Locutus. "He's exhausted,"
says Dr. Crusher. But he's telling them how to destroy

the Borg vessel before they assimilate everybody.
There are many ways to awaken. Some are fatal.

Others will save you, if you can be saved, whatever
it means to be saved. Data figures it out quickly

and the cube ship explodes, leaving the Federation
safe and the members of the Borg collective

in a spectacularly less structured condition.

9.
I still don't know how to be myself and belong
to something at the same time, much less rest easy

where I am, however pleasant, however graced.
These days all I want to do is sleep, and eat,

and ride my bike for hours on the sweaty blacktops,
drain my water in the first ten miles, fog my glasses,

not bother to glance at the corn to this side,
the soybeans to the other, slow as little as I dare

at the blind corners where a pickup may be
blazing my way with its oblivious tons of doom.

Zen & Blacktop

If your name was Tom, you'd know what to name your cabin.

The bicycle breeze: a blessing, whatever the humidity.

Hum of the tires, buzz of the blacktop.

What sound does the wheel make when it's done turning?

What does the mindful biker notice? Wind, road, distance, speed, direction, traffic, weather, landscape, the mirror, breath . . .

The island has only ten roads, even counting the dead ends, and still I miss turns.

The mindful biker steers around the potholes, and sees the potholes coming, or so I do believe.

The little island runway tees with the road. The signs say *stay out, stop, look, caution*. Vehicles over ten feet tall are supposed to detour onto the other road, a mile west. The whole place seems deserted, but somebody must mow the grass.

Someday I'll say *fuck it* and ride headlong down the whole thing, just to do it.

Mindful is letting my monkey mind sway and glide and turn with the pedals, float and glow with the broad water as I swoop by, lean a little with the moored sailboats offshore.

How lovely still is the countenance of this earth, how earthy the sweat of my brow and my aging but strangely sturdy body as I slip and slice onward and lean to the easy curves and pass among the summer houses shut up already and the beach chairs waiting impeccably to be used or forgotten and the last slide of the island down to the wet seam where the land hesitates and then continues on its slow and obedient way.

Traces

> *That man standing there, who is he?*
> *His path lost in the thicket . . .*
> —James Wright, "Three Stanzas from Goethe"

1.
Mottle of snow all through the woods, rabbit prints
soon to vanish, saplings grown up between old tire tracks.

This way, that way? Scotch pine and sycamore.
In the hummocky, waterlogged meadow a slouched

black dog . . . dead? No, plastic. A real black dog
sniffs for traces, a hundred yards away. A line

of orange flags along the tree line, as if we couldn't
tell where the trees are, and a thin yellow wire.

The black dog and a white dog start to bark,
not at me. I'm almost disappointed.

2.
On such a day, in a January thaw, how to walk
is one problem, how to read this world another.

What to notice, to record, to imagine. There are paths
and tracks, some full of icy water. Open spaces

between the trees. A few brown leaves quiver
when all else is still. Long ago I read the claim

that our souls are *larger* than our bodies, and when
I pause, look up, around, something begins

to swirl and echo. It does not end at my skin.

3.
James Wright was drunk and mostly miserable
when he wrote his best poems.

Correlation is not causation.
Thank God for that.

4.
How to be smart enough to write a simple poem?
How much does the snow matter? The plastic bucket,

the rotted steel drum, the rusty wheelbarrow in the weeds?
The desire to turn for home. The desire to see more.

5.
The forty-foot fallen tree makes a very long bench.
Just beyond, the creek whispers over a lost limb.

All the branches break someday, Jim,
but they'll outlast both of us.

You knew that. It's all in the moments
we find, the moments we're given.

Last summer a one-legged jay hung around
our redbud tree for months, splashing

in the birdbath, sneaking up to the feeders
as though I might shoot him through the window.

Here, now, what spills from a culvert
made an ice sculpture like organ pipes,

like muscles rippling. Tomorrow
it will be water, and both of us gone.

On the Way to Denver

From above, the clouds are always white. Color
is a construct. Words are bricks & mortar, studs
& drywall. Methane is invisible to the human eye.

Even this little bit of Nebraska, which may be Kansas,
is more than I can take in, cloud-covered or not,
the neat plots of fields & roads, wheat already green,

woods along the rivers still blurred & gray.
The arrow of an airstrip pointed northwest. The key
to shalom is dismantling: racism, patriarchy,

oligarchy, capitalism, and the use of vast abstractions
as markers of the so-called real world. From above
the clouds are pale and pure as a vast range

of my mother's mashed potatoes. And now
they are rising to meet us, we will learn how thin
they are, how empty, how full. They will hold

us up, they will let us down, the wheels will shriek
& bite into the irrevocable tarmac, the harsh
& fine & gritty surface of our days.

Late Explanation

I write out of indigestion, out of dejection, out of disdain and
    despair for the greed and venality of Those People.

You know who you are. OK, maybe I'm one too.

Because I want to think I'm trying.

Because I'm lazy, because I hate talking on the telephone, because I
    hate meetings even when I love the people in the meetings.

Because I don't want to explain.

Because so much needs to be explained.

Because some days I only want to heap up all my explanations and
    set them on fire.

Because I hope for smoke with the clean scent of maple and pine.

Because my parents let me play with matches, at least when it was
    time to burn trash in the barrel out back.

Because during the revival meetings we were not often threatened
    with fire but frequently reminded of hell.

Because I rarely burned anything I wasn't supposed to.

Because I had to put dead chickens in a wheelbarrow and throw
    them into the incinerator.

Because in summer after five or six days in the pit they'd fall right
    apart when I picked them up by the leg.

Because in my childhood this is what passed for trauma.

Because I did nothing to deserve my good fortune.

Because when the gas blazed up and caught their feathers and their flesh, the smoke flared up and out the chimney, and the harsh smell of burning replaced the brutal stink of decay, I could go in and wash for dinner.

Soft Tissue

    (after "Good Bones," by Maggie Smith)

Pain is common, though we talk about it too little
or too much. Common as the tendons

in my rotator cuff—I strained or blew it out
trying not to fall on New Year's Eve, staying up

somehow, grateful but my right shoulder
screaming silently as I handed Joel the small things

I'd carried to his car, as I walked inside, my slippery
slippers gliding on snow. I know. It keeps me

up at night, makes me lie on the wrong side,
stabs at odd moments, but it's not so much.

For every bad shoulder there's a broken leg,
a cancer, six bad hearts, two thousand hands

and knees aching all day, all night. Once I asked
my class how many were hurting in their bodies,

right then, and all but three held up their hands.
I felt like a man who's lived his life in a soft cocoon,

oblivious, knees and hips and all the rest making
no great fuss while all around me friends and strangers

carried their secret aches and agonies, banked or blazing,
members of the secret club everybody has to join.

On the Condition of Rural America

1.
Oak pews hard as stone, plain walls, the clock ticking behind, where only the preacher could see. The preacher saying *Every head is bowed every eye is closed,* saying *Now is the time, if you feel God moving in your heart, if you are ready to surrender, if you are ready for His peace* . . . My eyes closed, my head bowed, awhirl, a hot stew of anxiety and confusion. What did I feel, what did I fear, what did I hear? If I raised my hand, if I walked to the front, what then? There would be questions, not unkind, but particular. What would I possibly say.

2.
I was more scared of going forward than ready for salvation, more frightened of the preacher's questions than of dying unsaved. And yet I was more scared of dying then, fifty years ago, than I am today. Kennedy was dead, Khrushchev was not. The missiles still trembled in their silos. The fields lay bare and black for months until the storms came, and then the snow blew like it meant to bury us all, ran for miles across the fields, assaulted the homesteads, an army with billions of tiny cold warriors. It piled between the buildings, blocked roads and driveways, white sand in all our gears.

3.
The schools and the churches were full then, but it took more and more acres to make a living, the tractors and the feedlots kept getting bigger, the farm kids had begun already to head off to the church colleges and the state schools, come out as doctors and sociologists, nurses and lawyers and business executives, instead of farm wives and farmers.

4.
Who wanted to be sitting in those hard pews at thirty, at sixty, at eighty, with the clock ticking down the seconds till your heart

clutches and sighs and gives it up once for all? I wanted even then to keep my eyes open, to keep my head up. I wanted to look out of the pebbly windows, across the winter-bare plains, past the little huddled towns with their church spires and grain elevators, look out and to the long slow line of the horizon and the brilliant endless lens of the sky.

5.
But then it was autumn, and dark. My head was bowed, my eyes were closed. The preacher's voice was not harsh and not loud. He only asked that I fumble somehow into my deepest coverts, find and expose the soft creature there who had no desire to be examined or touched or interrogated, who wanted only to unfold like a night flower in its own time, to breathe quiet as grass in the dark, to find its way in solitude from what it was to something else.

The Smaller Mysteries on a Winter Sunday Morning

> *I become a transparent eye-ball. I am nothing; I see all . . . I am part or particle of God.*
> —Ralph Waldo Emerson, "Nature" (1849)

> *"Grand stand plays" are an abomination. Let the Gospel be presented in a plain, straightforward, and spirited manner.*
> —Daniel Kauffman, Manual of Bible Doctrines (1898)

Some people I've known for thirty years still seem like strangers.

Some people I've just met seem clear and close.

R. told me he's started putting a little dark sugar in his stir-fries,
    the day after mine turned out edible but a little drab.

When people become converted, said Daniel Kauffman, *their nature
    assumes a child-like simplicity.*

The student's father across the table yesterday, grease in the creases
    of his fingers and nails, too far away for me to ask what he
    does without feeling like a condescending fool.

The other father muttered to his son all through lunch, passing on
    things he'd gathered like a proud successful spy.

No M. in the choir today, she's off tending to her mother, who
    seems increasingly freed from this particular space and time.

G. sits downstairs now, with his mother who calls 8 times a day,
    out of cookies or wondering where Darvin's been for so long.

H. is in hospice. J. is returning to PA without her husband and is
    grateful for our support.

I don't believe I've ever spoken to her.

The sermon title is "The Space Between Us." I'm in the balcony,
    not too close to anyone, though we're all in the same room.

*The metaphor of society as a body was not favored by those eager to
    change the current order,* the pastor says.

I think I'd rather be an eyeball than a toenail, a finger than a heel.

We don't have to become one big eye, the pastor says. Communion is the resetting of the bones of the body of Christ.

O Emerson, where art thou?

The most grievous [mistake] has been to mistake intelligence for spiritual power, wrote Daniel K.

I have my great-grandpa George's copy of his book.

He was a Mennonite preacher in the day when they didn't get paid, which Daniel K. says is as it should be. Maybe an offering twice a year.

His copy is little marked, but in the part on "Secret Societies" George underlined *Christ Himself testified, "In secret have I said nothing."*

My copy of Emerson is thatched with pencil lines. Transparent eyeballs, currents of the Universal Being. *In the woods there is perpetual youth. There is a crack in everything God has made.*

Some Sentences for a Man Who Won't Read Them

He was the star running back of the first great football team at
    Flanagan High, not long after the Last Good War.

When I was in high school his name was still on the record board
    for the 440—54.1.

Now he has a four-pointed cane, and one shoe with a brace that
    wraps his calf.

He always said his brother Jim had run 52.9 a year or two later.

Now he asks what the plan is, and asks again in twenty minutes.

He and Mom were king and queen of the first homecoming. They
    didn't dance, but already they were sweethearts.

Now Mom reminds him to use the back bathroom, and sometimes
    he remembers.

He taught me to throw and to catch, to buckle down, to carry two
    buckets of water for balance, to turn back and look for the
    buttonweeds we'd missed.

He planted straight rows for fifty years, got up early, worked till
    dark, napped in his chair when he could. He and Mom put
    six of us through college, tended thousands of chickens,
    gathered millions of eggs.

When they moved to town he still drove out every day to help
    Gary, ran the combine and the big tractors, hauled grain
    to town, cleaned and greased the tractors and implements,
    sorted tools and seed.

A couple of years ago Gary started to tell us about little accidents.
    Dad caught a bin with the end of the field cultivator,

punched a hole in it. He never quite got the six steps to
> start the newest tractor straight in his head.

With him I put a new roof on our first garage, sad and rickety as it was.

We stretched new carpet in the tiny house, scraped, painted. Mom
> was better help with the wallpaper, but he was good at
> everything else.

We traded off driving the run-down U-Haul all the way from
> Kansas to Bluffton, Gary and Mom and Marlyce and the
> kids behind us in the station wagon.

We hauled our secondhand furniture, plates and clothes into our new
> old house, made a long row of cardboard boxes by the street.

It poured the next morning, and they sagged in the rain like the
> saddest, smallest, oldest mountains ever.

Nice People

> *Writers aren't people exactly.*
> —F. Scott Fitzgerald

> *There was a band playin in my head . . .*
> —Neil Young

Yesterday a guy who knows Richie Furay,
late of Buffalo Springfield, let the whole internet
or at least my Facebook page know that
by his lights Neil Young is not that nice a person,
and that furthermore Richie Furay is indeed
a nice person. I've never been in a room
with Richie Furay or Neil Young. I don't really
doubt that Neil Young was mean and wrong
half a century ago when he blew off Richie Furay
and Buffalo Springfield. But I know for sure that
Richie Furay didn't change my life and Neil Young
did, singing in that high whine that should have
been pure annoyance but somehow wasn't,
playing guitar solos that stayed on the same note
longer than anybody else would have dared,
out of sheer nerve, ego, boredom, rage
or God knows what, solos I haven't heard
in years but still know by heart, songs about
heartbreak and disaster. *Down by the river,
I shot my baby.* Who the hell would do that?
Not Neil Young, surely. The song is not clear,
and more clarity would not improve it. Writers.
*Or, if they're any good, they're a whole lot of people
trying so hard to be one person,* said Fitzgerald,
who knew all about trying so hard. *I am a parcel
of vain strivings tied / By a chance bond together,*
wrote that poser Thoreau, chasing a loon
around the pond, never getting close enough
to please himself, but close enough to write

about it. Writers aren't people exactly,
let alone nice people. Guitars in need
of someone to play them and a big Fender
amp, or rock bands that broke up decades ago,
or channels for this voice, that voice. Listeners.
The banks of the river. Not the river.

Tablets

All I ever wanted was to walk at the head of this strong new tribe, to have everyone hush when I say to them, hush, to choose from all the wide forking paths which path we should take among the lilacs, the dogwoods, the maples and the violets and the birdsong, to hear the whisper of sandals in the new grass behind me and begin to wonder who is cold and who is tired, who is bored and getting sulky.

But to come safe to the windy table and ask everyone to sit and to bend to their tablets as if to plates of meat and bread. To hold my tablet open in the raw wind and wish for calm, for sun, know that soon I must rise and break silence as though it is mine to keep or destroy, as though what I think is what matters,

as though the trust of these children no longer children is something I deserve when I am the one who has brought them into the windy spring with no reasons or excuses, with nothing to eat and no fire to make, when Katie has pulled up her socks and Christina still has the violet between her teeth and Brett is still looking and writing though his arms are blue.

I wish I could stand like a tree and warm them but no, what will I do next, what now, I can wish if I want for less wind and more sun, I can listen as they speak their new words and say *yes, yes,* and say *now we can go* and rise with the rest and return to the warm room in the midst of my beautiful, temporary tribe.

Lessons of a Gentle Childhood

Under this skylight many lost things are visible.
I see the mighty black and yellow spiders in the iris beds

by the old garage, and feel not a shred of fear.
I could husk two dozen sticky ears of sweet corn

and pick two quarts of strawberries on my achy knees
without whining once. I could hit four baseballs

in a row under the maple trees and over the fence,
the only kind of home run that counts in my private game.

I could sit through the whole Sunday night service
in the stickiest dusk of July and not once imagine

committing the unpardonable sin, just to see
if anything would change. I could sing *Just as I am,*

thine own to be seven times through and never switch
to "Mr. Tambourine Man" in my head, never dream

of dancing neath the diamond sky, just as I am
thine own to be, silhouetted by the sea, without

a single plea, hey, hey, I am weary, play another song
for me, an old song that I've never heard, play it

smooth and loud and long, play "The Boy Who Listened
Too Hard," play "The Boy with Dirt in His Nose."

Play "The Boy with the Lousy Guitar in His Arms,"
play "The Boy Whose Eyes Are Still Closed."

ABOUT THE AUTHOR

Jeff Gundy grew up on a farm in central Illinois and studied at Goshen College and Indiana University, where he earned his Ph.D. He is Distinguished Poet in Residence at Bluffton University. His eight books of poems include *Without a Plea* and *Abandoned Homeland* (both from Bottom Dog, 2019 and 2015), *Somewhere Near Defiance* (Anhinga, 2014), for which he was named Ohio Poet of the Year, and *Spoken among the Trees* (Akron, 2007), winner of the Society of Midland Authors Poetry Prize. Earlier prose books include *Songs from an Empty Cage* (Cascadia, 2013), *Walker in the Fog: On Mennonite Writing* (Cascadia, 2005), winner of the Dale E Brown Award, and *A Community of Memory: My Days with George and Clara* (Illinois, 1996). Recent poems and essays are in *Georgia Review, The Sun, Kenyon Review, Forklift, Ohio, Christian Century, Image, Cincinnati Review, Terrain,* and other journals. A 2008 Fulbright lecturer at the University of Salzburg, he taught regularly at the Antioch Writers Workshop and Language of Nature workshops in Cuyahoga Valley National Park. Lynn Powell writes, "Impish, probing, and expansive, Gundy's poems reward the mind and replenish the spirit." Of *Wind Farm,* Scott Russell Sanders says "[Gundy] carried along from his rural upbringing riches of imagination that are abundantly displayed in these pages."

His web page is https://jeffgundy.com/

NOTES

"Little Bridges" is for Mary Szybist and her poem "How (Not) to Speak of God," and after Rilke.

"Stairway": Italicized passages are the words of poet and teacher Nick Lindsay (1927-2020), my first poetry teacher and an ongoing inspiration. The first was a frequent refrain, the second and third are from an inscription in my copy of his book-length poem *Esau Lanier: A Sea Island Prince*.

"Instructions for Surviving the Eclipse, the Merger, and the Flood" Sources include:

Luke Myers, Associate Professor of Physics, Bluffton University, Forum lecture, 4/2/24 (paraphrased)

Carlos Drummond de Andrade, "In Search of Poetry," *Uncommon Speech of Paradise: Poems on the Art of Poetry*, ed. Robert Hedin & Jim Lenfensty

Walt Whitman, "Preface" to *Leaves of Grass*

Jane Wood, President, Bluffton University, "Bluffton University and University of Findlay to join in historic partnership," email, 3/22/24

Jesus, "The Gospel of Thomas," 77

Ben Franklin, "How to Get Riches"

Claire Clay, Director of Public Relations and Enrollment Operations, Bluffton University, "Important reminders for the April 8 solar eclipse," Community Connection, 4/4/24 info@911cellular.com, "Campus Flooding," email, 4/2/24

Archibald MacLeish, "Ars Poetica," *Uncommon Speech of Paradise*

ACKNOWLEDGMENTS

I am grateful to these presses and their editors, who first published these poems in book form:

Poems from *Inquiries* are copyright © 1992 by Jeff Gundy. Reprinted with the permission of Bottom Dog Press.

Poems from *Flatlands* are copyright © 1995 by Jeff Gundy. Reprinted with the permission of The Permissions Company, LLC on behalf of the Cleveland State University Poetry Center.

Poems from *Rhapsody with Dark Matter* are copyright © 2000 by Jeff Gundy. Reprinted with the permission of Bottom Dog Press.

Poems from *Deerflies* are copyright © 2004 by Jeff Gundy. Reprinted with the permission of WordTech Editions.

Poems from *Spoken Among the Trees* are copyright © 2007 by Jeff Gundy. Reprinted with the permission of University of Akron Press.

Poems from *Somewhere Near Defiance* are copyright © 2014 by Jeff Gundy. Reprinted with the permission of Anhinga Press Inc.

Poems from *Abandoned Homeland* are copyright © 2015 by Jeff Gundy. Reprinted with the permission of Bottom Dog Press.

Poems from *Without a Plea* are copyright © 2019 by Jeff Gundy. Reprinted with the permission of Bottom Dog Press.

I am grateful as well to these journals and their editors for publishing the following poems, which first appear here in book form:

NEW POEMS:

Anabaptist Remix: Varieties of Cultural Engagement in North America: "Rumor of Wings" (as "Emblems of the Times")

Call and Response: Intersections of Poetry and Art (Pennington Art Gallery, Columbus, Ohio)*:* "Les Bar de PTT"

Christian Century: "Natural Theology in the Late Pandemic," "Little Bridges," "Why I Keep Shoveling the Cursed Driveway," "Ways to Fail to Change an American Mind, Even with a Solid Hook and a Bridge to Die For," "Running across the Pews," "Natural Theology in the Late Pandemic," "Sunset Hill, Father's Day," "Greasing the Plow"

The Curator: "Elegy for a Solid Man"

Drawing Near: A Devotional Journey: "Some Naïve Questions"

Hamilton Stone Review: "Bears," "The Guy with the Pumpkin on His Head"

Journal of Mennonite Writing: "Stairway"

I Thought I Heard a Cardinal Sing: Ohio's Appalachian Voices: "Report from an Interior Province," "Seven Ways of Looking at Raspberries"

Kestrel: "Afternoon with Wind, Brown Thrasher, and Dream of Flying"

Literary Guide to Appalachia: "The Skink Poem"

The Nature of Our Times (online): "Notes Pertaining to the Tempest," "Notes from Bliss Hall, or How It's Going," "Kingfisher, or How Certain Autumn Days Advocate for a Significant Realignment of the Human Project"

Poetic Toolkit (Wick Poetry Center and Cuyahoga Valley National Park): "Musclewood"

Poetry Salzburg Review: "Stairway"

Relief: "Property," "September Lament"

Slippery Elm: "Quicksilver Messenger Service, *Happy Trails* (1969)," "Sunday Morning at River Ridge Mansion," "Split in Three Movements"

"Quicksilver Messenger Service, *Happy Trails* (1969)" was a finalist for the *Slippery Elm* 2023 poetry prize.

St. Katherine Review: "Implicit Bias in the Wilds of Allen County, Ohio," "Purple"

THE OTHER SIDE OF EMPIRE:

Poetry Salzburg Review: "Translation"

Rhubarb: "Damp Ode"

THE TRAVELER PONDERS SOME RUMORS:

The Christian Century: "The Traveler Ponders Some Rumors That Have Reached His Ears," "Winter Walk with Hooded Crows"

The Cresset: ""Windy Walk with Espresso and Globalization"

Forklift, Ohio: "The Traveler Fails Kierkegaard Once and for All" (as "The Traveler Continues to Fail Kierkegaard")

Kestrel: "The Traveler Attends the Friday Evening Concert"

Mid-American Review: "The Traveler Encounters More Renowned Cities, Foreign Tongues, and Items of Historical Significance"

The Mennonite: "Items the Traveler Has Yet to Fully Reckon"

Slippery Elm: "Things Overheard, Observed, and Possibly Misunderstood"

Smite the Chimes: "The Indolent Professor Is Shamed into Uncertain Epiphany"

Terrain: "Palanga Stintas"

OTHER BOOKS BY JEFF GUNDY
PUBLISHED BY DOS MADRES PRESS

WIND FARM (2021)

FOR THE FULL DOS MADRES PRESS CATALOG:
www.dosmadres.com